Faith & FINANCES: In God We Trust
A Journey to Financial Dependence

A Christian Devotions Ministry publication

**Lighthouse Publishing
of the Carolinas**

Faith & FINANCES: In God We Trust
A Journey to Financial Dependence

Our mission is to publish inspirational products that touch the heart, minister to the soul, and glorify God.

Published in association with Lighthouse Publishing of the Carolinas.

Available direct from your local bookstore, online, or from the publisher at: www.FaithandFinances.us
Book Cover and Interior Design by Behind the Gift. • behindthegift.com

ISBN-13: 978-0-9822065-4-6
ISBN-10: 0-9822065-4-2

Printed in the United States of America.

Dedication

*Christian Devotions Ministry would like to **thank all** those who, through their prayers, financial giving and service, helped launch this book.*

Michael Leonard,
John Mann, Ron
& Janet Benrey, Bill
and Marianne Jordan,
M.D. and El McCue, Kitty
Sproles, Tim Sproles, Ann Tatlock, Miggy Krentral, Allan and
Terri Kelly, Yvonne Lehman, Andrea Merrell, Emme Gannon,
Jo Huddleston, Alton Gansky, John Riddle, Marlene Bagnull,
Vonda Skelton, Vernell Jones, Bennie and the boys, Pat's Bible
study, Eddie's Sunday school class, Keith Glover,
Virginia Smith,
Mark and Nancy
Pitts, Jonathan
Clements, Diana
Flegal and the Pencil
Box Crew, Gary
and Jenny Frady,
Velma Frady, Mary
and Todd Denman,
Susan Dollyhigh,
Eric Dollyhigh, Pam
Boney, Erin Thomas,
Danny Woodall,
DiAnn Mills, Eva
Marie Everson, and
Debbie McCoy.

Mark 10: 17-31

(The Message)

The Rich Young Ruler

As he went out into the street, a man came running up, greeted him with great reverence, and asked, "Good Teacher, what must I do to get eternal life?"

Jesus said, "Why are you calling me good? No one is good, only God. You know the commandments: Don't murder, don't commit adultery, don't steal, don't lie, don't cheat, honor your father and mother."

He said, "Teacher, I have—from my youth—kept them all!"

Jesus looked him hard in the eye—and loved him! He said, "There's one thing left: Go sell whatever you own and give it to the poor. All your wealth will then be heavenly wealth. And come follow me."

The man's face clouded over. This was the last thing he expected to hear, and he walked off with a heavy heart. He was holding on tight to a lot of things, and not about to let go.

Looking at his disciples, Jesus said, "Do you have any idea how difficult it is for people who 'have it all' to enter God's kingdom?" The disciples couldn't believe what they were hearing, but Jesus kept on: "You can't imagine how difficult. I'd say it's easier for a camel to go through a needle's eye than for the rich to get into God's kingdom."

That set the disciples back on their heels. "Then who has any chance at all?" they asked.

Jesus was blunt: "No chance at all if you think you can pull it off by yourself. Every chance in the world if you let God do it."

Peter tried another angle: "We left everything and followed you."

Jesus said, "Mark my words, no one who sacrifices house, brothers, sisters, mother, father, children, land—whatever—because of me and the Message will lose out. They'll get it all back, but multiplied many times in homes, brothers, sisters, mothers, children, and land—but also in troubles. And then the bonus of eternal life! This is once again the Great Reversal: Many who are first will end up last, and the last first."

How to Use This Book

The book you hold is not unique. The writers in this volume are no more or less gifted than the thousands of authors who write daily devotions. The words are merely heartfelt stories, lessons and the advice of others who have traveled the devotional journey. This book is a primer, a tool to get you started down the path toward financial dependence on God. Here are a few tips on ways to use this book.

First, as you study the verses look for promises, prayers and praises. If one speaks to you, highlight the verse. Claim it as your own.

Second, write the verse in your journal. Ruled lines are provided at the end of each devotion, but it is our prayer that God will speak to you in such a way that you will need more than a few lines to capture His words. Note the passages that touch your heart. Reflect upon them. Re-read them often. Then act when He calls.

Finally, pray God's promises back to Him. Prayer is a conversation, the intimate dialogue between the Creator and created. Every author loves to hear his words recalled, quoted and remembered. The One called The Word and Author of Life is no different.

Good luck on your journey. When you reach the

end drop us an email. We'd love to hear how God worked in your life through this retelling of the Rich Young Ruler.

❧

To take the *Faith* & FINANCES challenge,
read other's stories or download our free study guide
go to: www.faithandfinances.us

Forward

"Show Me A Man's Check Register And I Will Show You His Heart."

As a pastor I've heard that taught many times over the years. I've said it dozens of times myself - and I sincerely believe that it is true. Godliness is often displayed through a man's wallet. When you think of the godly people you've known in your life, it's highly likely that one of their greatest character traits was that they were generous givers to God and His people.

There is a direct correlation between a person's faith and their finances. This book is a testimony to that truth. Jesus spoke about money and material possessions more than he talked about heaven, hell, or prayer. He understood that there is a close relationship between a man's heart and his wallet. Jesus knew that one of the hardest, and last, things a follower could give to God was control of his finances. When God controls your money, it's a good sign that He controls the rest of you as well.

Why is it so hard for people to allow their faith and their finances to collide? Our selfish nature is one reason. The apostle Paul said that *"everyone looks out for his own interests, not those of Jesus Christ" (Philippians 2:21)*. We suffer from the core sin of selfishness. It often reveals itself in our purchases. Our greed comes out at the mall, the car dealership, or the home improvement store.

Amazingly, this is not unique to Americans. It is a universal problem. Author Ron Blue told the story of visiting a small, rural village in Africa. He asked a village leader to define their biggest problem. The reply: Materialism.

Blue was taken aback. He expected the answer would be lack of food, medical attention, or problems with neighboring villages. But materialism? These people had no televisions, cars, or satellite dishes. They had nothing that Westerners would associate with the "good life."

The resident explained his answer. "If a man has a mud hut, he wants one made out of stone. If he has a thatch roof, he wants a tin roof. If he has one acre, he wants two." Materialism is a disease of the heart. It has nothing to do with where you live.

When your faith and finances merge together, materialism, greed, and self-centeredness, begin to fade away which makes room for generosity, compassion, and selflessness - the character traits that make us more like Jesus. Ultimately, that's what this book is all about.

❧❦❧

Gene Jennings is an Associate Pastor at True North Church in Augusta, South Carolina and the author of *Laughing With Sarah*.

Contributors:

Gene Jennings, Jan Loy, Cindy Sproles, Yvonne Lehman, Joanna Shumaker, Eddie Jones, Sauni Rinehart, Sandy Bradshaw, Beverly Varnado, Ann Tatlock, Irene Brand, Cindy Rooy, Candy Arrington, Phyllis Qualls Freeman, Sandra M. Hart, Cathy Bryant, Leah Mix, Andrea Merrell, Danny Woodall, Shelby Rawson, Loree Lough, Jennifer Landsberger, David Loy, Pat Jeanne Davis, Kelli Regan, Kristi Buttles, Dr. Christopher Stocklin, Miralee Ferrell, DiAnn Mills, Susan Dollyhigh, Virginia Smith, and Tina Givens.

Chapter One

The floor vent rattled, spewing its stale, heated breath into the room. A florescent bulb flickered from an overhead light. The wall clock clicked. He stood at the corner of the desk reading the front cover of a magazine marketed to church pastors. Beneath the publication sat a bundle of mail bound by a thick rubber band: Utility bills, solicitations and glossy brochures from real estate brokers offering to represent St. Paul's Community Church on the odd chance the congregation decided to sell. He wished they would. He was already tired of the gossip coming from the building committee. If they wanted to add another building, fine, but don't ask *him* to help pay for it. He picked up the magazine and took a seat in a leather chair to wait.

Through the slats of Venetian blinds he watched cars

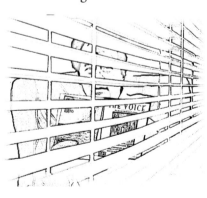 waiting to exit the church parking lot, heard the hum and whir of tires speeding past. Bunkers of crusty ice remained on the traffic islands from where the plows had cleared snow two days earlier. He hated winter, despised the short gray days. He was a beach boy, a man more accustomed to sandals and surf trunks than three-piece suits. But you couldn't

rent kayaks and surfboards forever. Not if you wanted to make a living.

Unhooking the top button of his blazer, he relaxed the pressure around his waist. A rubbery bulge sagged over his belt buckle. The dieting and treadmill had helped, but not enough. Maybe he should start swimming, though the chlorine burned his eyes. He flipped through the magazine. The door opened behind him and he started to stand.

"Don't get up."

He stood anyway, shook hands, and waited while the Pastor hung his tan overcoat on a hook behind the door.

Taking a seat behind the desk the Pastor asked, "So, how are you doing, Rich?"

"Fine."

"Just fine? Not good or great?"

"I wanted to talk to you about your sermon this morning. Give you a chance to apologize."

"Apologize? I'm not following."

"That part about planning for your financial future and how it's a waste of time. Was that meant to be directed at me? 'Cause it sure seemed that way."

"Believe me, Rich. My comments weren't specifically directed at you or anyone else. I was just putting the passage in context."

"I've given a lot of money to this church."

"I'm sure you have, Rich."

"My wife and I helped fund the first building campaign. Gave seed money when we didn't even have enough for ourselves. Check anyone who's been here awhile. They'll say,

'Rich and Peg have given a ton to this church.' 'Course, I'm sure that was the first thing you did when you got here. Check to see who the big donors were."

"I've never asked. Don't care to know. What's this *really* about, Rich?"

"I told you already. It's about you sticking to your business and staying out of mine. You want folks to give all they got to this church and not have a dime for themselves, that's fine. A man's got a right to his opinion. Just don't say something like that from the pulpit. Heaven and hell, Pastor. That'll preach every week, but stay away from my money."

"Your money?"

"You know what I mean. My clients' money *is* my money."

"Rich, I have to teach what's in scripture, you know that. I wouldn't be doing my job if I didn't."

"Then pick another passage. How 'bout those Beatitudes? 'Blessed are those that hunger, for they shall be satisfied.' That was a good series of sermons."

"Righteousness. 'Hunger for righteousness' is what the verse says. And besides, in today's message I didn't tell the congregation to give away everything they owned."

"That's what I heard."

"Well, you heard wrong."

"Excuse me?"

An awkward moment followed. Heat blew onto his ankles. Why did they have to keep it so hot in here? Why not knock the thermostat down a few notches and save money?

"Sorry. I shouldn't have put it that way," the Pastor said. "I was out of line."

"You got that right."

"Here's what little I know about money, Rich. I know that it controls people, that the lust for money and the fear of financial insecurity enslaves people. Paul was right. The root of *all* evil is the love of money."

"All I'm asking is that you stick to preaching about heaven and hell and let me deal with money matters."

"We're in the same business, you and me, just working different sides of the grave."

"How so?"

"You advise people on earthly wealth. I council them on eternal treasures."

"All I know is that I had two of my clients come up after the service and ask me about the tax benefits of donating a large chunk of their stock portfolio to the building fund. That's what I know."

Turning in his chair the Pastor opened the blinds. Cars idled in the parking lot waiting to exit. A bus shuttle van opened its doors and church members boarded.

"Heaven, huh? You really believe there is such a place?"

"I don't know. I guess. That's part of church isn't it?"

"Part of church?"

"You know what I mean."

The Pastor swiveled in his chair and looked at him. "Peg, what was her take on heaven?"

"Can we get back to what we were talking about? You know, my money."

"Not yours. His. And we'll get back to your finances but first I want to show you something."

"Is it gonna cost me?"

"Only every thing you have." The Pastor stood and walked to the door. "You'll need an overcoat. Take mine."

Chapter Two

Rich followed the Pastor up the sidewalk and across the parking lot to a split rail fence that divided the church property from a sprawling industrial park. On the other side of the drainage ditch, a row of paneled trucks advertised the latest in laminate cabinet tops. A halo of ice-encrusted snow encircled the vehicles. Rich reached the fence and pulled the borrowed overcoat tightly around him, trying to warm himself against the wind.

The Pastor stepped through an opening in the fence and, crunching packed snow beneath his shoes, jumped across the ditch. "You coming?"

Rich looked down at his black wing-tips, freshly shined just four days earlier in an airport outside of Atlanta. "Would have made more sense to drive, don't you think?"

"Where's the fun in that?"

Rich took two long steps and jumped, landing in the snow on the steep embankment. He grabbed the Pastor's hand to pull himself up.

"You hungry? The men and women of the Heavenly Banquet Ministry put on a killer lunch."

Rich looked past the back bumper of the truck and saw a row of serving tables being erected near the base of a loading dock. A woman in a white apron splattered with red sauce unrolled a long sheet of white butcher paper. She anchored the corners with porcelain plates, placing a vase of flowers in the center of the paper table cloth. Daisies in December. How quaint.

"Can we eat inside?"

The Pastor shook his head. "Insurance issues. They're fortunate to get the use of the parking lot. Come on. As soon as you get a bite of their spicy sausage rigatoni, you'll forget all about the cold."

Rich knocked snow from the tops of his shoes. "I doubt that."

He fell in behind the Pastor, taking small steps to keep from slipping on the ice and brushing against the truck. He still wasn't sure why he was traipsing across the parking lot on a frigid Sunday, two weeks before Christmas. He needed to be home catching up on correspondence. In a few days his clients would become consumed with shopping and holiday parties. Then he'd sit alone at his desk, reflecting on how quiet the house was without Peg. He missed her cinnamon and apple potpourri and the evergreen garland she used to hang on the banister. Maybe he should take a vacation. Go some place where he wouldn't be reminded of her absence every waking moment.

As if reading his mind the Pastor asked, "Rich, if God spoke to you and told you to go someplace, would you?"

"I guess it would depend on if it was really Him and where He wanted me to go."

"Forget the where and focus on the who. If you were sure it was God, would you?"

"I don't know. I mean, I guess. As long as I was sure it wasn't just some chemical imbalance causing me to hear voices in my head. I have to tell you, though, I'm not sure God talks to people like that. I know there are some who say they've heard God but they're usually standing at an exit ramp holding a cardboard sign and begging for money."

"So what you're saying, then, is if God called you by name and said 'follow me,' you'd tell Him that you'd have to get back to Him."

"Well, not in so many words, but yeah, I'd like verification. I wouldn't just up and leave."

"So, you're a man of facts first and faith second, is that it?"

"I don't believe in taking a blind leap of faith and hoping it'll all work out, if that's what you mean."

"But you *do* have faith? You believe in the stock market, for example, or else you wouldn't be in this business you're in. And you believe the advice you give your clients will make them money, otherwise you wouldn't recommend the investments that you do."

"Sure, but I've got years of experience and tons of evidence to back up my recommendations."

"But not faith in God?"

"That's different. You can't prove God. And you certainly can't calculate His stock earnings price based on an annual report."

"If that's the way you feel then why do you come to church?"

"'Cause I always have. And because church was a big deal to Peg. Look, I don't want you to think I don't believe in God. I do. I just don't think He's in the business of dictating our every move. He's there for the big stuff."

"And we're supposed to take care of the daily grind."

"Exactly."

"You loved Peg. Did she ever nag you about small stuff?"

"Some but not often."

"And did you? Do what she asked, I mean?"

"Usually. If it wasn't something dumb like going with her to a Clay Aiken concert."

"God faith is like that, Rich. It's falling in love and doing whatever the other person asks you to do no matter what."

They reached the loading dock. The Pastor paused at the bottom of a short flight of steps. "The thing is, Rich, no matter how much you think Peg loved you and how much you know you loved her, God loves you a lot more than that. And He *does* want to be involved in the daily grind. Think of the investment advice you give your clients and how it makes you feel when they take your recommendations and do well. Now multiply that feeling of satisfaction a thousand times and you begin to get a sense of how God feels when we turn to Him for our daily needs."

Rich looked around at the rows of tables and the crowd beginning to gather. He was easily the best dressed guest there.

"I thought we were going to talk about money, not my faith."

"How you worship money *is* a matter of faith. You can't separate the two."

"You mean like the homeless here who can't or won't work? Where's *their* faith?"

"Most of these people do work. They just don't make enough to feed their family. So when they get a chance at a free meal they take it. And no, they're not above accepting a handout when it's offered. You want iced tea or soda?"

"I'm good with water."

The Pastor poured from a plastic pitcher.

"Rich, a little faith *hopes* God will do what He's promised. Big faith *believes* God will do what He's promised. But, great faith *knows* He already has. Take our lunch guests today. They arrive every Sunday expecting to get fed. A lot of them walk from the shelter because they can't afford the bus fare. They *walk*, Rich, regardless of the weather, because they know that when they arrive they'll get a hot meal and all the seconds they want. That's faith. You believed like that once. I know you did because you told me some months back about how you sold your boat to buy Peg that house she'd always wanted. Would you say that was a mistake?"

"No, but I miss that boat every day; I really do. Not the upkeep, mind you. That got old quick. And I don't miss those hot days on the water when there was no wind. But I miss those evenings anchored out in a small creek, looking up at the stars. We'd planned to go cruising on that boat. I'd dreamed all my life of sailing to the islands and surfing while Peg painted those little sunset portraits you see hanging in restaurants down in the Caribbean."

"Do you miss that boat and that dream more than you miss Peg?"

"Of course not. I wouldn't trade those last few months with her in that house for a fleet of mega-yachts. She loved that place. Especially her garden."

"And you loved watching her work in it."

"Well, sure. Tending to those plants on her good days was the only thing that got her through those treatments."

"But when you sold that boat you weren't sure you were doing the right thing. I know because you told me of how stepping off that boat the last time nearly broke your heart."

"It was a bad time to sell. I took a huge loss on the deal and I knew the couple that bought it would never take care of that boat the way I did. Plus, land prices were going through the roof."

"But you did it anyway."

"For Peg. Not because it made sense."

"That's what I mean, Rich. The things God asks us to do don't always make sense. Not at first, anyway." The Pastor looked onto the loading dock and waved to a woman carrying a tub of lettuce. "Stay right here. I want you to meet someone."

The Pastor bounded up the steps leaving Rich alone at the table. He glanced at his watch, then back at the church parking lot. He really didn't have time for this. He'd scheduled a conference call at 2 p.m. with a stock analyst in New York and he'd already had to postpone the meeting once. He wished now he'd just gone to his car and ignored the business with his clients and the Pastor's sermon on the Rich Young Ruler.

"Janet, this is Rich. I want you to tell him what you told our mission board the other day."

"You mean about why we do this? Sure. But first I need to take your order. What are you in the mood for? " She flipped open an order pad.

"Whatever they're having is fine with me," Rich said, glancing at the others.

"That runs the gamut. Just about every one here orders something different."

"So it's not just a buffet of greens and meat?"

"Heavens no, Hon. We got some of the best chefs in the city cooking for us. Just because we eat outside doesn't mean the food has to be low grade. Tell you what. How about if I get you a menu?"

"Hey, I know that guy," Rich said. "He used to service the copier machines in our building. What's he doing hanging out with this bunch?"

"He's probably asking himself and God the same question. You see, money takes on the color of its owner's heart, and sometimes we don't know who we really worship until we're standing in a serving line at a homeless shelter. He's turned to the only One who can help, or is willing to help."

"Seems to me that if he'd done like you've been saying and had more faith he wouldn't be standing out here in the cold."

"Rich, God would rather teach us His ways and change our character, than provide for our every need. By coming here each week, your copier friend is stretching his faith. He's depending on God. Here, this might explain it better."

The Pastor handed Rich a mole-skin, leather-bound journal with ruled lines.

"A diary?" Rich asked. "You want me to read someone's diary?"

"Devotional journal. Our guests, some of them anyway, have learned what we all come to realize eventually. That there is no such thing as financial independence. Only financial dependence on God."

"See, there you go again."

"Wealth weighs us down more than debt, Rich, you know that. Just look at how little time you have for the things that matter. When was the last time you didn't worry about the market, your portfolio or your client's investments? I've yet to see a rich man truly at peace unless his hands are open and giving to others. As soon as he clinches his fist and tries to hold onto what he has, his face frowns. Anyway, just read the first few entries and let me know what you think. Lately, with the economy the way it is, we've received a lot on poverty and provision."

"I'll bet."

"You stay here while I help set up the rest of the tables. Then, as soon as we get everyone seated, we'll say grace."

Rich sat, pulling the overcoat tightly around him. Opening the journal his eyes fell on the words, *Secure Investment Strategies God's Way*. He began to read.

Secure Investment Strategies God's Way
Jan Loy

*"Who then is the faithful and wise servant, whom the
master has put in charge of the servants in his household
to give them their food at the proper time? It will be good
for that servant whose master finds him doing so when
he returns. Truly I tell you, he will put him in
charge of all his possessions."*
Matthew 24:45-46

In these days of turbulence in the economy, it seems everyone is cautious about what to do or what not to do. Even the so called "experts," the financial planners and stock portfolio managers, offer conflicting advice as to what to do. No one can predict what tomorrow will bring.

Now more than ever, it is important for believers to remember that the Lord has planned a secure investment strategy for us. It is safe and is sure to bring returns.

This strategy is not as much about money as it is about the mind set and actions of the individual. God's word calls us to be people of faith and integrity in every circumstance. He calls us to be salt and light in this world. He calls us to invest in the things that make a difference.

Here are some steps that will lead you to a higher return on your investments:

Invest in a positive outlook. Limit your exposure to the media. All the "breaking" news tends to produce an excessive amount of dread, fear and anxiety. Instead, stay informed without overdoing it. Choose to remind yourself of the blessings you are experiencing today.

Express your gratitude to the Lord and to others. An attitude of thankfulness will help anchor your thinking on the things that matter.

Invest in the lives of those around you. Share your knowledge with others. Volunteer to teach or coach. Mentor someone. Encourage those who have a passion for the skills you possess. God has graced you with talents. Share them.

Invest in relationships. Cultivate friendships. Take time to make a call or write a note of encouragement. A smile is the gift that gives back, so give yours away.

Invest in your spiritual growth. Spend time in prayer. Study God's word. Meditate on His truth. Claim His promises. Pray the prayers found in scripture. Examine the way others in the Bible have praised God. Share the Lord's love with a Bible study group. Continue to give financial gifts to help further the work of the Lord.

When we are faithful in attitude and action, remembering His ways, He will help us through the turbulent times and we will bless others along the way.

PRAYER
Lord, give me insight to invest in the things that honor You.

BUILDING BLOCKS OF FAITH
He who sows righteousness reaps a sure reward.

❧ *Faith* & FINANCES ❧

Journal

Getting Your Bucks in a Row
Cindy Sproles

*"Therefore I tell you, do not worry about your life, what
you will eat or drink; or about your body, what you will
wear. Is not life more important than food, and the body
more important than clothes?... So do not worry, saying,
'What shall we eat?' or 'What shall we drink?' or 'What
shall we wear?'...But seek first his kingdom and his
righteousness, and all these things will
be given to you as well."*
Matthew 6:25, 31, 33

I peered through a crack in the blinds and, for a
minute, I imagined I was at the fair—the mailman, a
duck in a carnival game, and I held the pellet gun to
knock him over. "Pow, pow!" I said, blowing imaginary
smoke from the end of my finger.

Through our financial disasters I wondered if we'd
ever see the light of day. This was the worst kind of
torture. A bill from the power company, a late notice,
and a disconnect notice. So many bills and so little
money.

We'd prayed earnestly about our finances. The
money we owed wasn't from lavish spending but the
creditors didn't care about the how's, only that they got
their slice. I couldn't sleep, couldn't eat and I had an
impending desire to smash the phone when it rang.
God knew our situation. *Why was He turning his back
on a family of six? Lord, won't you provide?*

Our financial situations are not always caused from
bad choices—sometimes the unexpected happens. And
when we're in so deep that escape seems impossible, we
wonder how we'll manage.

 Christ said, "...do not worry about your life, what you will eat or drink; or about your body, what you will wear... seek first his kingdom." I'd done nothing but worry. God was telling me to seek Him first and then all these things would be added.

 When our finances spin out of control, it's easy to lose sight of our priorities. Things become distorted, we lose track of the spiritual order of life. We call to the Father as an after-thought, as a rescue, instead of seeking Him first—in the natural order.

 I scooped up the last envelope and tore the paper. A money order dropped to the floor from an unknown provider. It was exactly what we needed to pay the bills. God had provided fully.

 God doesn't always drop money from an envelope. Many times His provisions come in ways to cope with the situations we face. More times than not, the answer to my financial provision hasn't been cold hard cash; rather it's been a way to save, the courage to sacrifice something that isn't necessary, or simply a calm peace. He cares for the birds of the air, He cares for me. We need not worry. He'll help us get our bucks in a row.

 Seek Him first and He will provide what is appropriate.

PRAYER
Father, I know you use my money or lack of it to test me. Help me trust you for my daily bread.

BUILDING BLOCKS OF FAITH
How we spend our money reflects the priorities
in our lives.

Journal

_____
_____
_____
_____
_____
_____
_____
_____
_____
_____
_____
_____
_____
_____
_____
_____
_____
_____
_____
_____
_____
_____
_____
_____
_____
_____
_____
_____

The Romance of Hard Work
Yvonne Lehman

*"Unless you are faithful in small matters, you won't be
faithful in large ones."*
Luke 16:20

In the 1980's, Inspirational Romances were really going
strong and I was writing for two companies, Zondervan
and Thomas Nelson, so I quit my job. At the time, I had
two mainstream and several romances published—on my
way to fame and fortune. Well…not exactly. Suddenly, the
financial rug was pulled out from under me. The market
became flooded with romances, some of the books were
being criticized, and both companies ceased publishing the
romances.

There I was with a husband, four children, and bills
that were accustomed to being paid with two incomes.
Now there was only one income. We coasted into poverty
as I tried to be published in other genres but was rejected.

The survival instinct is strong and we'd become
accustomed to eating, so I had to pray…and find a job.
The only one I could find immediately was as a desk clerk
at a conference center—making minimum wage, which
was $3.20 an hour. Other desk clerks were high school
students working during the summer or weekends, or
those without education or skills for other jobs. I felt it
was beneath my skills and certainly not a job to further my
career as a writer. Part of the job required being nice and
friendly to the guests.

Well…I felt out of place. I was supposed to be doing
something creative, wasn't I? Well, in my spare time I began
color coding the different conferences, planning ahead for
check-in to make things easier. I began talking to guests

and heard some really interesting stories. And…on payday, I thanked God I could buy groceries for the family.

Bible verses popped into my head. *Be thankful in all things. Study to show yourself approved, a workman that needs not be ashamed.* I became ashamed…of me and my self-righteous, egotistical attitude and asked God's forgiveness. I, with the help of God, would make the best of things. Hey, soon I got a 20-cent raise.

Sometimes the inn had small conferences. I had free time after guests checked in. I only needed to be there in case anyone wanted anything. I asked my supervisor if I could write in my spare time and she said "yes," as long as I did my work. I began to write and started taking one course at a time at the university.

I began to love that job, the beautiful inn, the people I worked with and the guests. For the next few years I helped support my family, wrote a couple of books, and earned my Master's Degree in English Literature. After that, I taught a class, one night a week for the college associated with that conference center, and they paid me $40 an hour—as much as I made working an entire week as desk clerk.

The lesson I learned was to be content in my situation, serve God and others, and look for what great things God will do…if I have the right attitude and work toward my heart's desire. I learned there is no small job when it's done for the Lord. And He blesses.

❖

PRAYER
Lord, when my financial stream runs dry, help me to hear your voice calling me to deeper waters elsewhere.

BUILDING BLOCKS OF FAITH
When we are faithful with our money, God entrusts us with His heavenly riches.

Journal

_____
_____
_____
_____
_____
_____
_____
_____
_____
_____
_____
_____
_____
_____
_____
_____
_____
_____
_____
_____
_____
_____
_____
_____
_____
_____
_____
_____
_____

A Little Faith in a Big God
Joanna Shumaker

*"… for your Heavenly Father knows that you are
in need of all these things."*
Matthew 6:32

$10,000! Letters and phone calls from the hospital collections department demanded we pay immediately. I was struggling to make sense of the insurance forms, hospital and doctor bills, while recovering from a major surgery. We'd fought the insurance company to pay over $500,000 in bills and I wondered why we still had to fight them for the remainder, seemingly small in comparison.

We began to pray, asking God to intervene and take charge of this situation. A month later, our answer came in the mail—a letter from college friends who'd heard about my surgery and our financial struggle to meet the medical bills. Their kindness led them to send us the gift of prayer and an envelope with a check for $10,000. God had provided.

I could just hear the Father saying, *"O what little faith you have! Did you forget that I know all these things and will care for you?"* In my Bible, Matthew 6 is appropriately titled, *"The cure for anxiety."* God gives us all the hope we need in that one small section of the Bible. He shows us how small our cares and worries are in comparison to His care and supply for us. Whether it's money or material goods, God can provide these things, just as He takes care of all His Creation.

If you are struggling with anxiety over medical bills, house payments, future plans, or strained family relationships, God gives hope and peace in this short passage of scripture that will calm the heart and turn your focus toward Him. Just as He took me into His Hands, He'll take you as well. Look for the ways God shows His care for you everyday, then trust Him to take care of all the rest.

PRAYER
Father, in times of need help me to lean on you for every dime.

BUILDING BLOCKS OF FAITH
Our lack of money is just as much an answer from God as His abundance.

Journal

Manna to a Full Meal
Eddie Jones

"On the evening of the fourteenth day of the month, while camped at Gilgal on the plains of Jericho, the Israelites celebrated the Passover. The day after the Passover, that very day, they ate some of the produce of the land: unleavened bread and roasted grain. The manna stopped the day after."
Joshua 5:10-12

On the fourteenth day of the month, while sitting at a corner table at my favorite restaurant, we celebrated my birthday. We spoke of dreams for the future and recalled the good-old-days of the past. We reminisced about boats, beaches and snowboard trips to the mountains and how much fun it was traveling with the boys when they were small.

You know, back when we used to have money, jobs and health benefits.

I wondered, though, as we looked back, if the past was really as good as it seemed. If we're not careful, the good-old-days will cast a shadow over today, dimming our view of tomorrow.

That was the problem the Israelites faced the first time they approached the Promised Land. They'd come to believe their days of slavery in Egypt were the good-old-days—that God's promise of protection and provision was for yesterday and last year, not today and tomorrow.

When they questioned their future in His hands, God's anger burned against them.

Contempt. That's how God views our skepticism. We may call it "exercising sound judgment," a "crisis of confidence," or "good old common sense," but God calls it what it is: unbelief and sin.

Whatever your present financial circumstances, God already knows your need, just as He knew the needs of the Israelites when He led them out of Egypt, and to the edge of the Promised Land. He knows your debts, bills and job status. He understands the giants you face—and sees them as gnats. God can provide and will, but we must make an effort to manage our financial situation responsibly. Then trust. Believe what God promises.

On the evening of the fourteenth day of the first month of the year, the Israelites ate their last meal of manna. The next day God's miraculous blessing of daily provision vanished and the Israelites began to feast again on unleavened bread and roasted grain. Once more they would work for their daily bread by the sweat of their brow.

Christ says, *"Stop doubting and believe."* Believe, indeed. The good-old-days are not in the past. They're just around the corner.

PRAYER
Lord, I know of your great deeds. Help me to know your ways.

BUILDING BLOCKS OF FAITH
Trust God, not His methods.

Journal

Nightly News and Our Daily Needs

Sauni Rinehart

My God shall supply all my needs, according
to His riches in glory.
Philippians 4:19

I don't watch the news any more. Why should I? It's just the same old depressing headlines over and over. This bank has failed. These people have lost their homes. That CEO has destroyed his company—but still gets his six (or seven!) digit bonus.

It's enough to make you want to close all your accounts and hide your money under the mattress. Issues and questions about money and finances circle us like vultures. Sometimes it's easy to let fear and uncertainty take over.

What do we do when the reality seems to be contrary to what the Lord says? He says He'll supply *all* our needs. What do we do, though, when "supplying needs" in our society means a job, and we've received a pink slip? Or what if an unexpected expense comes in that we just don't have the funds for?

We have to trust.

I know, I know. This is one of those "Christian" answers, too good to be true. It's naïve. It's unrealistic.

But it *is* true. We just have to trust.

Recently, I experienced the truth of Paul's words in Philippians. My mother-in-law, Ruth, was terminally ill and in a skilled nursing facility. While hospice was paying for her medical care, the facility required payment for "bed and board" expenses, costs that insurance doesn't cover and money we didn't have.

Keeping her well cared for was our top priority, but we didn't know where we'd find those funds. We'd need thousands of dollars that she—or we—didn't have. We looked at options. Could we take out an equity loan? No, the value of our home had dropped too much to do that. Should we raid our retirement funds? The penalties were prohibitive. What were we going to do? Ruth needed care. We needed money to pay for that care.

So I prayed—a lot. Then I trusted that God would supply this very important need.

And He did. God provided through an unexpected source of income that covered Ruth's care for several months. In fact, He'd set the wheels in motion for this gift *before we even knew what the need would be.*

I don't know what your need is. But God does. He's promised to provide food and shelter and clothing—those are your *needs.* Trust Him. Pray to Him. Be confident that He'll do just as He's promised. Because He will.

PRAYER
Father, help me to have a grateful heart regardless of my circumstances.

BUILDING BLOCKS OF FAITH
God would rather teach us His ways and see our faith increased, than to provide for our immediate needs.

Journal

_____

_____

_____

_____

_____

_____

_____

_____

_____

_____

_____

_____

_____

_____

_____

_____

_____

_____

_____

_____

_____

_____

_____

_____

_____

_____

Moving to Manhattan... Kansas
Sandy Bradshaw

"Do not worry about your life, what you will eat or drink; or about your body, what you will wear. Is not life more important than food and the body more important than clothes?"
Matthew 6:25

I thought I was pretty trusting when, at the age of thirty-seven, I encouraged my husband to leave the corporate world and move our family of five to Manhattan … Kansas. He wanted to earn a degree in Bible Ministry and become a full-time Pastor. I wanted to trust God.

Our home sold quickly for a good profit. We were able to buy a less expensive home and avoid house payments while he was in school. My husband's company gave him a generous bonus and our savings account added to the financial assets we took with us.

There were several married couples with families starting classes that fall. On one of our first Sundays to attend church in our new hometown, another couple from the school with two grade school age boys, sat in front of us.

By this time, most of the moving boxes were unpacked and the house was in order. Unlike my usual routine, which was to sleep-in and barely get out the door on time, I'd gotten up early that Sunday, fixed a dessert and had dinner in the oven so that when we got home from church it would all be ready. Just before the end of the service, I leaned over and asked Mike about inviting the couple home for lunch. He agreed and, when the service was over, the Weatherston's accepted our invitation.

We had a pleasant meal. The adults got to know each other better while the kids played. As they were leaving, Doug and Sally thanked us for inviting their family to lunch. They told us they had been so blessed by the worship service that when the offering plate was passed they wanted to give something, but the only money they had was what they needed to buy lunch for their family. They decided to give the money anyway and trust the Lord to provide. Lunch with our family was God's response to their act of faith.

Our new friends, Doug and Sally, took Jesus at His word when he said…*"Do not worry about what you will eat or drink….look at the birds…they do not sow or reap….yet your heavenly Father feeds them. Are you not much more valuable than they?"* We were humbled by their faith and challenged to deepen our own trust in the Lord.

Perhaps the provision your neighbor needs is in your cupboard.

Even when your faith is sometimes shallow, believe in God and trust in His promises to care for you, your family, and for those around you.

PRAYER
Lord, help me to pray less for my daily needs and more for those of my neighbors.

BUILDING BLOCKS OF FAITH
Don't worry about the work to which you've been called. If God is calling you to a task, ask and He'll provide.

❧ *Faith* & FINANCES ❧

Journal

_____

_____

_____

_____

_____

_____

_____

_____

_____

_____

_____

_____

_____

_____

_____

_____

_____

_____

_____

_____

_____

_____

_____

_____

_____

_____

Documenting Our Daily Provision
Beverly Varnado

*"Your love O Lord, reaches to the heavens, your
faithfulness to the skies."*
Psalm 36:5

My husband pointed to a box of my journals spilling
on to his side of the closet, "What are you going to do
with these? They're in my way."

What was I going to do with them? Could I possibly
get rid of my journals?

When he left the room I stooped down to crack one
open, scanning the entries. Inside were stories of God's
provision in my life, the accurate recording of God's
faithfulness. In one area, finances, He'd demonstrated
over and over His abundant provision. On one page, I'd
recorded the words of the Psalmist who declared God's
faithfulness and told of how it reaches to the skies. In
other words, it is immeasurable, without limit.

There were entries covering the time I was concerned
over whether or not we would have to sell our house
because I wasn't generating income. Today, fifteen years
later, we still live in that same house.

Another volume contained a prayer request about
paying a large sum of back taxes due to an accountant's
mistake. It took a few years, and we still don't know
where the money came from, but we finally paid off the
debt. In a more recent journal I expressed anxiety over
how we would pay the mounting medical bills due to
a string of health crises. Again, in time, the statements
from the hospitals and doctors finally stopped coming
as the amount due columns all turned to zeroes. Across
the years, so many prayers have been answered.

My husband wonders what I am going to do with these journals. Why, keep them, of course. Maybe not on my husband's side of the closet, but keep them close I will. And something else I will also keep, and that is what God taught me through them—that He is faithful. Immeasurably faithful.

PRAYER

Lord, thank you for your faithful provision in my life. Thank you for your persistence in teaching me to trust you. Thank you that with you even the sky is not the limit. In Jesus' name. Amen.

BUILDING BLOCKS OF FAITH

Never doubt in darkness what God has whispered to you in the light.

Journal

_____

_____

_____

_____

_____

_____

_____

_____

_____

_____

In His Time
Ann Tatlock

"He hath made everything beautiful in His time"
Ecclesiastes 3:11

As I stood at the window looking out at the gray
November morning, I felt the jittery fear and anxiety
of the past year gel into a hard lump of resignation.
Fourteen months had passed since my husband's business
partner walked out, leaving their fledgling business
in financial ruin. Scrambling to scrape by ever since,
Bob and I faced a December that looked worse than
bleak. There would be no way we could pay our bills,
let alone buy Christmas gifts for family and friends. *And
if the downward spiral of economic bad news continues,* I
thought, *surely we'll lose everything.*

I turned on the coffeemaker in the kitchen, then
padded back down the hall in my slippers to my office.
No one else was awake. This was supposed to be my
quiet hour for Bible reading, but God had let me down.
Jehovah Jirah, the God who provides, had somehow not
provided for me.

I switched on my computer and opened my e-mail.
There was a note from my friend Kris, a talented painter
who lives in New England. Kris and I had never met,
but she'd written to me after reading one of my books a
couple of years earlier. We'd become fast friends via the
Internet, regularly exchanging family news and prayer
requests. At the time we connected, her own husband
had been out of work, so she knew what it was to face
financial uncertainty.

"I hope you won't be angry with me," she began,
"but last February I held a show, and I dedicated the

proceeds of the first painting sold to you...."

As my eyes slid over the words, I couldn't quite comprehend them. I had to read her note several times before I finally understood. Kris had sold a painting and she was sending me the proceeds—because the Lord had laid it on her heart to do so! She had tried to think of a way to send me the money anonymously, but couldn't decide how. "So," she confided, "I simply have to trust that you'll know the money isn't from me but from the Lord."

"You may remember," she went on, "how, when Mike was unemployed, money came in to us from unexpected sources. It lifted our faith so." She explained that the woman who had bought the painting had only now paid for it and, "it's just sad it has taken so long."

While Kris felt frustrated by what appeared to be the buyer's procrastination, I was awed by God's perfect timing. We hadn't needed the money in February so much as we needed the money now. Kris didn't know that, but God did. In a rush of wonder, I jumped up and paced the house, marveling at God's glorious provision. Fifteen minutes earlier I had despaired, and now I rejoiced! Who but God could bring about a change like that?

The Lord not only knows *what* we need, He knows *when* we need it. He is Jehovah Jirah, and his timing is always perfect.

❦

PRAYER
Lord, help me to trust your timing in every area of my life.

BUILDING BLOCKS OF FAITH
When you pray about your needs, watch expectantly for God's answer.

❧ *Faith* & FINANCES ❧

Journal

Chapter Three

The temperature began to drop; the wind increased out of the north. Clouds thickened; flakes fell. Slowly at first, and then faster. The tar-black pavement of the parking lot, freshly plowed the day before, turned pewter gray, then white.

Rich closed the journal and shoved it under his plate. What was he doing out here? He had a conference call in a little over an hour and now that it was snowing traffic would be a mess. Three men began unloading poles and bolts of plastic. Rich hurried to help.

"So, what'd you think of our little notebook?" his Pastor asked, taking one corner of the tent. "Pretty deep stuff, huh?"

Rich wondered how the man could stand the cold, especially with the wind gusting the way it was.

"They've been through a lot, that's for sure. But no more than most, I guess."

"You got that right. Life happens to us, regardless of our faith. The difference is how you react to tough times. Who you give your problems to."

"I see, now, why they call this the Heavenly Banquet Ministry. If this was the only real meal I got each week I'd walk for miles, too."

"Would you?"

"I haven't always been this well off. Peg and I struggled, too. We got tossed from our first apartment because we fell behind on the rent. It was a two-room unit. Kitchen and living area in one room, bed and bath in the other. When the neighbor across the hall snored I had to turn up the volume on our TV. Then the gas station where I worked switched to self-serve pumps and I lost my job. Peg, she was still in school; had one more semester. Our landlord cut us some slack but he had to make a living, too. A friend let us live in the basement of his parents' house while they were out of the country, but we were never sure when the couple would return. It got pretty dicey at times. Looking back now, it was kind of fun. Not legal, but fun."

"So then you understand how God allows situations to develop so He can teach us His ways while providing for our needs. Like free meals each Sunday."

"Nothing's free, Pastor."

"This is. Everything you see, the food, staff, this tent. It's all paid for with contributions. Our church, plus some others, support the Heavenly Banquet. Most of the money comes from individuals who tithe to this ministry."

"I tithe at church."

"Do you now?"

"You think I don't? I thought back in your office you said you didn't check how much someone gave."

"I don't. I'm just wondering if you give the full ten percent?"

"Depends. Are we talking before or after taxes?"

"Doesn't matter."

"I'll bet it does to the finance committee."

"But probably not to God. I don't think He cares what accounting system you use. Some take ten percent on their gross earnings because they know that even though taxes are taken out of their check, those taxes also provide services like roads, security and social programs like Medicare and Medicaid. So for them, it's right to take the tithe off the full amount. Others find it more convenient to tithe the net income. But again, I don't think God cares. He looks at the heart and your motives, not your tax deduction on your income tax returns."

The men assembling the poles moved into position

and Rich, along with the others, lifted the tarp. He could smell a sourness in the wind, the odor of unwashed men and soiled garments.

"Sure you don't want your coat back? You look cold."

"Let's get this tent up, first."

"So the Old Testament laws about tithing don't apply anymore?"

"God was teaching us how to rely on Him. That's the main lesson we need to learn. But He wants us to obey and follow Him out of desire, not duty. If the only reason you're giving money to the church or some ministry is because of guilt or to meet some obligation you made to a church budget or building campaign, then stop. God doesn't want or need your money. He loves a generous giver, not a grumpy one."

"I'm not sure that's something you want to say too loud from the pulpit, Pastor. You preach that and you could end up like our guests here, waiting in a bread line."

"You know? Maybe that's not a bad idea. I could teach on the fruits of generous giving. Start out with the basics of tithing and then move into lessons on stretching our faith and money. Maybe I could use you as an example."

"Me? How?"

Two men holding one end of the frame snapped the tarp in place, pulled it taut and then, taking the pole from Rich, set it in place.

"Wait here."

Rich watched as his Pastor approached the other guests. Every so often he'd gesture toward him. Rich began to feel self-conscious. He stepped under the tent, flipping up the collar of the overcoat. A dusting of snow fell down his shirt.

The Pastor returned with a wad of cash. "Here."

"What's this?"

"Your daily provision. Notice the slogan over the word ONE."

"'In God We Trust.' Yeah, I get it, Pastor."

"Do you?"

"Look, I have money. I don't need this."

"You might later. Now, tithe ten percent and keep the rest."

"This is dumb. Why didn't you just take the tithe out before you gave it to me?"

"Because that's not how it works."

Rich sighed and counted the cash. He handed a fist full of bills back to the Pastor. "What do I do with the rest?"

"Keep it. And hang on to the journal, too."

"Why? I thought it stayed here with the ministry."

"Sometimes it travels. There's a section in there about tithing. Some pretty radical stories that I think you'll find interesting. But I will need my coat back. My work here is done."

"Aren't you staying for lunch?"

"Can't. Got a plane to catch."

"So, you bring me over here, take up a donation for me from people who are broke and then you leave? I thought you wanted to show me something important?"

"I did. All of them are important," he said, gesturing toward the guests. "Plus, I wanted you to see how this ministry operates. It was her idea, you know."

"Who?"

"Peg's. She's the one who dropped off a basket of vegetables one morning and told me to give them to someone in need."

"My Peg? She never said anything to me about that."

"I think for her, working in that garden was God's gift. The harvest was just an afterthought. Anyway, she was the seed that launched the ministry."

"I always wondered why those plants never produced any more than they did. I just figured she had rabbits or deer eating the plants."

"Giving from the heart, Rich, and doing it with joy."

Rich removed the overcoat and handed it back. He was about to step under the tent and take his place at the table when the Pastor said, "Hey, you want to come with me?"

Rich stopped and turned. "With you? Where?"

"Central America. I'm leaving for a ten day mission trip. Interested?"

"Thanks. No."

"Ah, come on. God just gave you, what? A couple hundred dollars? That's more than enough for a week down there."

"I don't do mission trips. Peg, now, she went all the time. Loved helping with that Appalachian Mountain Project. But I never could get excited about sleeping in tents and bunks with people who only bathe occasionally. Reminds me too much of Boy Scout camping. Plus, there's my job."

"You think the stock market is going to tank because you miss a few days from work?"

"The market? No. My clients' investments? Maybe."

"Here's the thing. We had a doctor drop out; an unscheduled surgery came up. But he's already paid for his plane ticket. I can call the airlines and get the ticket changed but I'd have to do it right now. The flight leaves Reagan National at 4 p.m. Want me to call?"

Rich glanced at his watch. "That's in less than three hours."

"I can swing by and pick you up. It'll take me about forty-five minutes. Have to grab my bags and change, first."

"I wish I could, Pastor, I really do. But I can't just

take off without letting my clients know I'm leaving. Plus, I have a conference call I'm supposed to be on this afternoon. I've been trying to nail down a time with this analyst for months."

"Call on your cell. Once we get checked in you'll have plenty of time at the gate before we board."

"I don't know. Doing something like this just doesn't feel right."

"That's because you're not in control. You haven't had time to analyze, plan and execute the strategy."

Rich cocked his head and studied the Pastor.

"I majored in business before going to seminary. I understand how the risk versus reward ratio thing works. Trust me, the payoff on this trip will be huge."

"Maybe next time."

"Might not be a next time, Rich. We're not promised tomorrow, only today. Like I said earlier, the only reason there's a seat available on the trip is because one of our doctors had to go in for emergency surgery this afternoon. A fifty-two year old patient keeled over while pushing his boy up a hill on a sled. So you just never know."

"What if I can't get a good cell signal in the terminal, then what?"

"You can use the Captain Club lounge. I have guest privileges."

"This is crazy," Rich said.

"No, it's stepping out in faith. Pick you up in forty minutes. Just make sure you bring the journal. That'll give you something to read on the plane. And pack light. You're going on an adventure, not a vacation."

Chapter Four

At a half-past 4 p.m., Sunday afternoon, a crew of baggage handlers sealed shut the luggage compartment of a TransAmerican Airlines flight bound from Washington's Reagan National to Managua, Nicaragua. Rich sat in coach class between a young Hispanic male listening to music through headphones and a chubby call-center operator from Gaithersburg who, just that morning, had broken up with her boyfriend. Rich leaned forward and smiled at the Pastor who sat across the aisle

"I've never done anything like this. Never ever," the woman said, turning toward Rich. "It's not like me to just buy a ticket and leave, but you know what? I'm tired of planning every little detail. I mean, where's that ever gotten me? Dumped for some bleached-blonde-hair stylist, that's where."

Rich stared straight ahead at the royal blue fabric of the backrest eighteen inches from his face. He hated flying coach; hated flying period. But on those rare occasions when he did, he went first class. Some years ago the airline industry, in an attempt to maximize profits, had shrunk the leg room in coach. A computer model matched to social behavior had determined that eighteen inches of leg space was the minimum amount passengers would accept before they grew restless. Rich was way beyond restless. He was anxious and quickly sliding into panic mode. *This was stupid. Flying out of the country like this without notifying his clients.*

"We had it all planned," the woman continued. "We

were going to get married next May and then, wham. He tells me this morning that I'm too controlling, too manipulative. Not spontaneous enough. I'll show him spontaneous. You don't mind me talking like this to a complete stranger, do you? I hope not. I usually don't go on a talking jag unless I'm about to start crying. You ever been to Central America? This'll be my first time. I'm catching an eco-tour group and we're going to see a volcano. I can't wait. If I can get close enough I'm going to throw my ex-boyfriend's picture into the cone. When are we going to pull away from the gate? I'm so ready to be away from this place."

Rich wasn't. He wished, now, that he'd declined the Pastor's invitation and stayed at home, but no. He'd thrown some clothes into a knapsack, grabbed his passport and bolted down the front steps wearing just a loose-fitting poncho and the pair of khaki slacks he'd worn when he'd painted the front porch railings. Had he known they were going to postpone his flight, he'd have taken more time to pack.

Without wanting to appear too concerned, he turned toward the woman. "I know how you feel. If they were going to delay our flight and hold us at the gate, they could have at least let us stay inside the terminal."

She didn't answer. Only turned toward the window and sniffled.

Rich reached under the seat and unzipped the front pouch of his knapsack. He pulled out the leather journal and, still leaning forward, saw his Pastor wink at him from across the aisle. Turning to the journal he began to read again.

Of All I Possess
Irene Brand

"One thing you lack," he said. "Go, sell everything you have and give to the poor, and you will have treasure in heaven. Then come, follow me."
Mark 10:21

During His earthly ministry, Jesus advised His followers how to consider their possessions. In the parable of the Pharisee and the tax collector, the Pharisee boasted, "I give tithes of all that I possess." I believe he was telling the truth because tithing was one of the most important tenets of the Hebrew faith.

In another translation the verse reads, "I give a tenth of all I get." How many members of Christian churches can truthfully say that? From experience, I judge that it's probably a small percentage. I've been treasurer of our local Baptist church for several years and during that time, I've learned more about the giving habits of some members of our congregation than I want to know. In some instances, those with the lowest income are more faithful in tithing than those who are financially well off.

I've read that Jesus taught more about stewardship than he did about eternal life. I've never checked to see if that's true, but He was very definite in his instruction about the way Christians should consider their possessions. The incident with the Rich Young Ruler illustrates that Jesus requires *all* that we have, not just a tenth.

When we read that Jesus told the young man to sell all of his possessions and give the money to the poor, most of us shrug our shoulders and say (or think), "So! That doesn't apply to me. *I'm* not rich!" Compared to most of the population living in other nations, we are. But even if our bank account is lean, we're tempted to accumulate greater wealth and more possessions.

When Jesus asked the young man if he had kept the commandments, He referred to the last six only, which explains how we are to deal with one another. The young man had kept these commandments, but he had missed the larger point. Jesus looked into the heart of the man and realized that he had made wealth his god. His possessions were more important to him than anything else. They were his security. This doesn't necessarily mean that Jesus expects us to give away all of our possessions and become a burden on others. He's indicating that anything which comes between us and God has to go if we want a close relationship with Him.

Do you consider all that you own *yours,* or do you believe it belongs to God? We can never fully be in the will of God until we consider ourselves stewards instead of owners of our material possessions. There *is* a cost to discipleship but in the end, the cost is small compared to the riches of living in His kingdom.

Give. The gain is great.

***

PRAYER
God, make our will, Your will as we consider what you've entrusted to us. Amen

BUILDING BLOCKS OF FAITH
It's not a matter of how much you possess but how much your possessions matter to you.

Journal

_____
_____
_____
_____
_____
_____
_____
_____
_____
_____
_____
_____
_____
_____
_____
_____
_____
_____
_____
_____
_____
_____
_____
_____
_____
_____
_____
_____
_____

Channeled Tithing
Cindy Rooy

"… and of all that you give me I will give you a tenth."
Genesis 28:22

Does God ever have fun? Does He enjoy surprising His children with gifts?

Watching sports and movies helps my husband and me unwind and often provides our entertainment. We acquired a tiny, hand-me-down, black and white TV when we were married. We appreciated having that set, but longed for a new 25" color console television. Unfortunately, we couldn't afford one.

As we debated using our tithing money, Jim resolved to remain faithful in giving the church 10% of our paychecks. He kept praying for ways to make additional money and eventually an opportunity presented itself at work. The executives' cars were being auctioned off. If Jim could get one particular car, he would do some body work and resell it at a profit. He submitted his bid and was notified the next day that he won.

Hours later, an executive informed Jim that the car used to be his and he wanted to keep it. The man was out of town and missed the bidding, but offered Jim $200 for the right to purchase the car in his place.

After thinking about it, Jim declined the offer. We needed more than double that amount to pay for our TV. Surprised, the executive asked why we rejected his proposal and Jim revealed our plans for the kind of television we desired.

"Let me get this straight. You don't even want the car, but you're buying it to make a profit in order to purchase a TV?"

"Yep," replied my husband.

"Would you please follow me to my office? I have something you'll be interested in."

Jim accompanied the man to the top floor and watched him remove from his desk drawer a portfolio of color console TVs.

Giving it to Jim he said, "If you let me buy that car with your bid, you can have your choice of one of these televisions. All you have to do is go to the warehouse to pick it up." His brother was a Zenith dealer.

We loved our new TV and learned that the principle of giving back to God, recorded in Malachi 3, is still true today. God not only blesses those who trust and obey Him, He is creative in surprising us. How has God gifted you for tithing?

PRAYER

Lord, thank you for your faithfulness to us. Help us to trust you completely as we manage our money.

BUILDING BLOCKS OF FAITH

God has promised to provide what you need, so examine your core concerns and ask for His goodness.

Journal

_____

_____

_____

_____

_____

_____

God's Trash is Greater than Our Riches

Candy Arrington

"For I am the Lord, your God, who takes hold of your right hand and says to you, 'Do not fear; I will help you'"
Isaiah 41:13

I sat in the church parking lot—a tithe envelope in one hand; a checkbook in the other. The finance office was about to close. Tomorrow heralded a new year. My head and heart were at war—should I write a check for the amount necessary to complete our tithe for the year, wiping out our checking account in the process?

I closed my eyes, *Father, I'm sorry. We've been unfaithful. We've let other things take priority.* My mind drifted over the course of the year—unexpected out-of-pocket medical expenses, car repairs, college tuition, an expensive vacation planned the year before, purchases of things we wanted but didn't really need.

And the tithe check was always written last.

You never charge a late fee, Father, or send a past due notice. Overwhelmed by God's compassion and mercy, and my unfaithfulness, tears flowed. *Trust me,* His voice whispered.

I pulled a pen from my purse and wrote a check for the full balance of our checking account, sealed the envelope, opened the car door against the whipping wind, and made my way across the parking lot and into the church. Although I knew I was doing the right thing, nagging doubts plagued me. How would we function until our next check arrived?

Pulling into the driveway at home, I got out and

opened the mailbox. As I sifted through the stack, a return address caught my attention—my publisher. I jumped back into the warm car and ripped the envelope open. Inside was a royalty check that was almost enough to cover our expenses until the next pay check. *Thank you, God!*

Further down in the stack was a package. Enclosed were two books I had contributed stories to almost three years before. I'd given up on ever receiving copies.

Once inside, I threw away the remnants of the package along with junk mail. But every time I walked by the trashcan, I felt uneasy. *That's silly. It's just trash.* But the feeling wouldn't go away. Finally, I fished the package out and looked inside. A folded piece of paper was wedged in one corner. I took it out and gasped. It was a check for $200. Laughter rippled inside me and spilled out my mouth. *Father, not only do you provide, but you're so creative about it. How could I ever doubt you?*

Our sinful human nature tells us to hold on, be tightfisted with our money. We fear what lies ahead. But God whispers, *let go. Trust me. Then you will know my ways.*

❧

PRAYER
Father, help me to trust you no matter where you lead.

BUILDING BLOCKS OF FAITH
Worshiping wealth is merely serving a smaller god.

_____

_____

_____

_____

_____

_____

_____

_____

_____

_____

_____

_____

_____

_____

_____

_____

_____

_____

_____

_____

_____

_____

_____

_____

_____

_____

_____

_____

_____

_____

_____

Rent-to-Own? It's all His
Phyllis Qualls Freeman

*"A tithe of everything from the land, whether grain from
the soil or fruit from the trees, belongs to the LORD;
it is holy to the LORD."*
Leviticus 27:30

Dad fussed and fumed as he slipped off his work shoes. He had the habit of taking his shoes off and padding about the house in his stocking feet. That night Dad sat at the kitchen table drinking a cup of coffee, recounting the trouble he'd experienced with his rental property. For the third time that year a family of renters had just moved out.

"They left the house dirty. Those old green garbage cans were overflowing, and junk is scattered around the stupid yard," he told Mother. "I've spent all afternoon cleaning so I can rent it again." Why couldn't he keep renters?

In Dad's second property, the renters seemed to stay put. Mother managed that property and when Dad questioned Mother about what she did that was different, he was surprised by her answer.

"Irvin, I tithe on the profits from my rental," she said.

Dad mumbled as he rubbed his chin and pondered her unexpected statement. He was not quick to change his ways, but he said he'd think on it.

Leviticus calls us to tithe on everything, not just our weekly paycheck. That tenth of any profitable thing already belongs to God. The tithe is hallowed and not to be considered lightly. Giving is an act of our worship and obedience.

Mother believed in God's blessings on obedience. She'd learned early in her Christian life to tithe. Even though Dad was not a believer, he noticed that whatever Mother did seemed to be blessed, including the home she managed for him. He finally figured she had favor with God as she tithed.

When Dad purchased a third rental, he said, "Eva, you can tithe on the profit from this house too, if you'd like."

Because I heard my mother speak of the joys of tithing, I never felt that it was a debt I owed, nor a burden to slip that check or money into an envelope and drop it into the offering plate. Tithing and giving offerings are joyful privileges. My gift to God.

Have you thought about the tithe as something holy, a *sacred* or *blessed* offering? God has given us an abundance of blessings. Isn't it time you give back and say "Thanks" to Him?

PRAYER
Lord, are my possessions helping or hindering my testimony for you?

BUILDING BLOCKS OF FAITH
It is more difficult to be faithful in plenty than in poverty.

Journal

_____

_____

_____

_____

_____

_____

_____

_____

_____

_____

_____

_____

_____

_____

_____

_____

_____

_____

_____

_____

_____

_____

_____

_____

_____

_____

_____

_____

_____

_____

Tithe on a Salary of $15.00 a Week?

Irene Brand

"And of all that you give me I will give you a tenth."
Genesis 18:22

I was fifteen years old, and I was euphoric. I had gotten my first job! Five days a week, $15.00 per week. My euphoria soon suffered a setback, though. My oldest brother came home for a visit. He was impressed that I'd joined the work force, but his thoughts, in my opinion, took a radical left turn when he asked, "Have you started tithing yet?"

Tithing? On a salary of $15.00? How much would $1.50 each week further the Lord's work?

I'd been a Christian for a few years, but had never earned my own money. I was annoyed with my brother for even bringing up the subject. I sulked. What gave him the right to tell me what to do with my money? My brother and his wife went home, but he'd sown the seed.

I believe if an idea comes into our mind that we absolutely cannot forget, then God is probably calling us to speak that word, do that good deed, or immerse ourselves more strongly into our worship.

Obedient to the wooing of the Holy Spirit, I started tithing on my small salary. Even several years ago, $1.50 a week wouldn't have made much of a splash in the Christian ministry. The point was not what that meager offering did for the Church, but what the discipline of tithing did for *me*.

A few years later, I met the man who was to become my husband of over fifty years. Not only was he a Christian and a member of the same denomination I served, but he also tithed. During the years of our marriage, we have tithed on our income *before* taxes were deducted. And believing we don't really *give* until we've exceeded the ten percent, we contribute a great deal more than a tithe to the Lord's ministry through our local church.

We've also been faithful in other areas of service, and God has blessed us abundantly. It's often said that a person can't "out give" God. It's been true in our lives. We have never lacked for anything. Our health has been good, and we've had many other blessings because we have heeded His call. No, *God* doesn't need our tithe. *We* need *God's tithe* in our lives.

PRAYER
Our Father in Heaven, may we have the strength and wisdom to listen to the still, small voice that prompts us to do your will. Amen.

BUILDING BLOCKS OF FAITH
Our level of provision depends upon our calling and the culture in which we work.

Journal

_____

_____

_____

_____

_____

_____

_____

_____

_____

_____

_____

_____

_____

_____

_____

_____

_____

_____

_____

_____

_____

_____

_____

_____

_____

Chapter Five

Rich finished reading the last devotional and looked up. As he did a flight attendant leaned down and spoke to the Pastor.

"Great," the woman sitting next to him said. "Now they're de-icing the wing again. At this rate we'll never get away. You know I once sat on an airplane for five hours before they cancelled our flight. I hope that's not what's going to happen today. But you never know. It's like once you step aboard you lose all rights. One time I was flying back from someplace, I can't even remember now, and our plane left late because the pilots and crew needed more time to sleep. Can you believe that? Never even updated the departure time. Just let us stew in the terminal while the crew slept. The airline industry is major whacked if you ask me."

Rich hadn't and wasn't about to. As the flight attendant walked back toward the front of the aircraft his Pastor unbuckled his seat belt.

"Finally we boarded," she continued. "All the time I kept thinking that since it was the airline's fault we were leaving late they would hold our connecting flight, but no. When we reached Atlanta and got off I found out my connecting flight had just taken off. Of course, this was after we'd parked at the end of the terminal for twenty minutes waiting for an available gate. I'm pretty sure the slot we got was from the connecting flight that left."

The Pastor stood and opened the overhead bin, pulled his backpack from the shelf and slung it over his arm.

"So I literally sprinted through the Atlanta airport trying to catch the tram and you know what they told me when I finally reached a ticket counter? That all the flights to D.C. were sold out. They couldn't find a single airplane they could put me on. Not one. But here's the best part. Those passengers who'd paid more for their ticket, they got on standby and got home. But not me because I'd shopped around and purchased my ticket online at a steep discount. You know what they gave me? Nada. Nothing. Wouldn't even help with the car rental. I swore then that would be the last time I'd fly. But look at me. Here I am again, sitting on a plane. Just shows how stupid we are sometimes."

The Pastor closed the overhead bin and turned, resting his elbow on the armrest in front of Rich as he leaned down.

"Rich, I have to take a call. There's a chance I might miss this flight. Then again, from the looks of things, the plane might not ever get off the ground, anyway."

"What happened?"

"You know Dick on the Trustees Committee? The flight attendant just said someone from the church called. Dick died this afternoon."

"I thought he was getting better."

"Guess the cancer spread faster than they thought."

Rich unbuckled his seat belt and started to stand. "I'll go with you."

"You can't. Once you board you can't leave. FAA rules. The stewardess had to get her supervisor involved so I could step off to call Dick's wife."

"You want to borrow my cell?"

"Better use the lounge." He cut his eyes past Rich and over at the woman sitting by the window. "And I might still be able to make the trip. It'll just depend on when the funeral is. But don't worry. I'll make sure someone's waiting for you in Managua."

"Can't you just tell the stewardess I'm traveling with you?"

"You can't back out now. I already told the team you were coming. They're counting on you. Besides, it's not like this is a surprise to God. So just trust Him to take care of things."

"Him I trust. It's this airline that has me concerned."

The Pastor smiled, started for the front, and paused. "There's a hotel across the street from the airport with a cyber-café so if there's no one to pick you up, check your email."

"What if they won't let me use their computers? What if their Internet connection is down? Is there someone I can call when I arrive?"

Without looking back, the Pastor waved off the questions and exited the aircraft.

"Look, they've finished de-icing the wing," the woman said.

Rich stared out the window. Beyond the aircraft and across acres of gray pavement and snow-covered grass, the Woodrow Wilson Bridge spanned the black waters of the Potomac River. He felt a jolt. The ground crew pushed them away from the gate and the whine of the turbines increased.

From far away he remembered Peg's voice and the way she'd looked into his eyes as she laid in the hospital. "Rich. Don't worry. It'll be all right."

He thought about her picture in his wallet. The one he'd taken of her sitting on the stone wall overlooking the harbor in St. Thomas. Unzipping the side pouch of his knapsack he pulled out his passport and placed it on his knee. Then he dug past two Granola bars, a toothbrush, toothpaste and a small bottle of aspirin. He reached the bottom of the pouch. No wallet. He felt his back and front pockets. Empty. *Think. Where did you last have it?*

He remembered standing beside the conveyor belt as they were going through security. He'd placed his knapsack on the belt and, emptying his pockets, dropped his belongings into the gray tub. Passport, ticket, reading glasses … but not his wallet. Now he remembered. He'd slipped it inside the Pastor's backpack to keep another passenger from stealing it.

The thrust of the engines threw him back in his seat. He shot a quick glance back at the terminal. They bumped and bounced down the runway, angled skyward and disappeared into the clouds.

Chapter Six

The woman next to Rich began to sob. Rich wanted to cry, too. In all his years he'd never traveled anywhere, much less out of the country, without his wallet. Now, here he was flying to the second poorest country in the Western Hemisphere without cash, credit cards or even the name of someone he could call when he landed. He sat with his head braced against the backrest, eyes closed, wondering what he should do. His neighbor tapped his shoulder and pointed across the aisle.

A woman sitting beside the Pastor's empty seat leaned out and said, "That man who got off before we left, I think he forgot this." She handed Rich a well-worn guidebook. "You two were traveling together, right?"

Were, Rich thought. *But not anymore.* Rich thanked her and looked at the front cover. The Lonely Planet's Official Backpacker's Guide to Nicaragua. *Great*, thought Rich. *An instructional manual for the lonely and lost.* He stuffed it into the magazine pocket on the seat in front of him.

"May I see that?" asked the woman sitting next to him. "I didn't even think to bring one."

"Knock yourself out."

Rich handed her the book. As soon as he did he regretted the decision. Skimming the guide would have given him something to read. He opened a copy of the in-flight magazine but found his eyes wandering over the pages without any comprehension of what he'd read. Rich put the magazine back and reached beside his hip, pulling out the leather journal. He was tired of reading the woes and wows of others who'd found their faith strengthened by trials, but what else was he going to do for six hours? Nap?

Flipping through the pages at random he found a single passage scribbled in the margins of the journal.

"Call upon me in the day of trouble. I will deliver you. You will glorify me."

Right. Like that's going to happen. The longer he studied the words, though, the more he felt drawn to pray. Something he hadn't done in a long time. *The man and woman next to me will probably think I'm just napping anyway. They don't have to know how scared I am.* Resting his hand on the pages of the journal, he closed his eyes.

"O Lord, I need you now. Deliver me to my destination. Be my wings. Be my guide. Be my eyes, Lord. Be my mouth. Don't leave me alone and lost."

The prayer didn't help. His mind raced, worried about what he'd find when he landed. He would arrive after dark. He knew little about Managua. Only that it was Nicaragua's capital city and a poor and dangerous place. He spoke no Spanish, didn't have a hotel reservation and didn't even know the name of the team he was to meet. All he had was his knapsack and the guidebook. And the journal. *Maybe God's speaking to me through their stories. I'm not the first to find myself scared and alone. No, of course not. Happens all the time. Happened to Peg, in the end.*

He opened the journal and began to read.

Facing Our Fears
Sandra M. Hart

*"I will lie down and sleep in peace, for you alone,
O Lord, make me dwell in safety."*
Psalms 4:8

Our church recently took a group on a mission trip to Honduras. My interest was piqued as soon as I heard about the trip. When I found out where Honduras was located in Central America, I knew we would be flying across the Gulf of Mexico. I was afraid of flying over the water. It goes back to watching the movie Jaws and possessing an overactive imagination. I didn't know if I could force myself to board the plane.

After a bit of soul-searching and prayer, I decided to trust God and sign up.

Though I ignored the fear, it never went away and the taunts of well-meaning friends didn't help. "If the plane crashes into the Gulf, we'll all go to Heaven at the same time," they quipped. I wasn't comforted.

I took a window seat and watched as the city of Houston grew small. *Oh Lord, what am I doing?*

Fear tried to seep in but a good book and a lot of prayer helped to occupy my mind. I only allowed myself an occasional peek out the window. There was nothing but blue—blue sky, blue water—an unending canvas of blue. When I saw the beautiful curves of the Honduras shoreline and a thin line of white sand leading directly into a green mountain landscape, I relaxed. God had given me a gift by allowing me to concentrate on other things as we flew over the ocean and, when the plane soared over the shoreline, I realized He'd nudged me to show me He'd kept His word.

I had the window seat on the flight back. I watched

a movie, glancing out occasionally. When I saw the Texas shoreline, I felt God saying to me, "See, I got you here safely. I can take care of you." God wasn't accusing me because I had this overwhelming fear. He comforted me instead, allowing me to see that He was able to make me dwell in safety as the scripture says.

Fear lives in the mind but grows in the heart. When I turned my thoughts to Christ, He cleaned the worry from my mind.

If you have fears that are keeping you from doing important things, like serving, trusting and following God, pray about them. As you face your fears, let God work in your heart and mind. You'll find that God's love is bigger than all our fears.

PRAYER
Father, I know fear is faith in Satan. But your word says love conquers fear. May it be so in my life.

BUILDING BLOCKS OF FAITH
Living by faith proves to us and others that God is real.

Journal

_____

_____

_____

_____

_____

_____

_____

A Shortcut to the Long Way Home
Cathy Bryant

*"When Pharoah let the people go, God did not lead them
on the road through the Philistine country,
though that was shorter."*
Exodus 13:17

"I'll follow you," I called out through the car window. His car pulled onto the highway and I fell in behind, staying close to his bumper. But after a few minutes, I wondered what I was thinking following this fool.

There has to be a better way, I thought. *Where is he taking me? Is he lost?*

A few miles down the road I called him on my cell. "Shouldn't we have taken that last exit?" He told me to relax and hung up.

As I drove along, certain that it wouldn't be "fine," I realized my walk with the Lord was about as anxious and confusing. I looked at how I'd failed to follow Him during times of crisis and I felt ashamed.

I thought of how often I'd questioned God, asking Him if He knew what He was doing. Sometimes I find it difficult to trust that His way is best and too often I try to go my own way, thinking that surely I know a better way. For me, the shortest and quickest route seems the best.

But that's not always God's preferred path for His children.

When Pharaoh let the children of Israel leave Egypt, God took them on a path that didn't make sense, on a route that left them exposed, vulnerable and scared. With their backs against the Red Sea, and the Egyptian soldiers in front, they cowered, demanding to return to the safety of slavery. But God told them to rest and wait. He would reveal His glory and power if they would only trust Him.

God hasn't changed. He still leads his children in ways that seem to make no sense. Sometimes He intentionally places us in perilous positions. He does this to see if we'll trust Him and to show us His awesome and amazing power. Trusting God proves to us and others that He is real.

I learned later that if we'd taken the exit we missed, we'd have gotten caught in a traffic jam. Road construction had closed two lanes. In the end, the long way was the shortest route.

If the path you're on seems bewildering, learn to trust that God knows what He's doing. Offer Him praise for working in your life in magnificent ways. Thank Him that He's willing to use you to make His glory known. Those who follow God will find themselves going places and doing things they could never accomplish on their own.

PRAYER
Thank you, Lord, that you are willing to make your glory known to the world.

BUILDING BLOCKS OF FAITH
When you follow God's leading you'll find yourself doing things you couldn't possibly do without His help.

Journal

_____

_____

_____

_____

_____

_____

_____

_____

_____

_____

_____

_____

_____

_____

_____

_____

_____

_____

_____

_____

_____

_____

_____

_____

_____

_____

_____

It's Light Time
Jan Loy

"Come…let us walk in the light of the Lord."
Isaiah 2:5

While walking in my neighborhood one evening, darkness came sooner than I expected. All at once, I was walking on a familiar sidewalk, but in total darkness. I reassured myself, knowing this was my regular morning walk route. Suddenly, I tripped and almost fell, not seeing a bump in the sidewalk. Then a low hanging branch slapped my face. Things certainly became more complicated in the dark!

Up the hill, straight ahead were street lights. I quickly moved toward those lights. As I got closer, my vision improved. The bumps and cracks in the sidewalk were more distinct, the trees were clearly visible. It was amazing what a difference light made in the journey!

The experience that night is similar to our journey in life. There are many times we walk through the routine, familiar things, not expecting dark times. Yet confusion comes and suddenly, our way seems lost. We find ourselves tripping along, unable to see clearly. Fear and uncertainty mark our steps.

During those times it is good to remember to head toward the Light. For in His light, safety and clarity can be found. The Lord is always faithful to shine His light to illumine the way…we just need to walk in it!

I have found that His light provides:
Direction
Hope
Encouragement
Correction
Strength

When we walk in His light, we learn to trust Him. We can set aside fears and enjoy the journey. Look for His light and walk in it today!

PRAYER
Father you search the earth to strengthen those whose hearts are faithfully committed to You. May it be so with me.

BUILDING BLOCKS OF FAITH
Where God guides, He provides.

Journal

_____

_____

_____

_____

_____

_____

_____

_____

_____

_____

_____

_____

_____

_____

_____

Set Aside for a Season
Leah Mix

"For I know the plans I have for you, declares the LORD, plans to prosper you and not to harm you, plans to give you hope and a future."
Jeremiah 29:11

Have you ever been in a "holding pattern" in your journey through life? It is emotionally draining to wait, not knowing if or when you will be able to get moving down a normal path again. Did you find it painfully uncomfortable?

This is where I am right now. God has chosen to allow me to "sit out" of many social gatherings, as I have developed a severe reaction to fragrances. I can have a mild form of the sniffles, or a go-to-the-hospital-by-ambulance-episode that has proven to be life threatening. For a social butterfly and church worker bee, this malady has clipped my wings drastically. The recent holidays, Thanksgiving through New Years have been a real adjustment, especially sitting out most events.

Living in my bubble I call my home, I have had to relearn my use of time. Books and crafts can only fill so many hours and I have to admit, discouragement and doubt try to creep in. Thankfully, the Holy Spirit revealed the truth of His Word again, making it clear this is part of God's perfect plan for me. It is for this season in my life and it is for my good and His glory.

Isn't it refreshing when a truth you have heard in the past, seeds itself deep within your spirit and gets you going again on a path, even if the path is only one step at a time? He purposely doesn't show us more than we need to know. That's where faith comes in.

If you, like me, are currently going through a "holding pattern," ask God to reveal His "today plan" to you. You may be surprised at what He'll have you doing. To be sure, I am.

God will never lay out your whole life's plan for you to see and then let you walk down a path, unhindered by obstacles. No, He is much too creative for that. Chances are, you will see your neighbors and others in a whole new way, for it may be you He is using to encourage or to bring them to Himself. One thing is for certain; you can count on the fact that each day will be a series of faith-filled steps with a promise. "I know the plans I have … to prosper you … to give you hope and a future.

PRAYER
Lord, reveal the plans You have for me. Plans to prosper me, plans to give me hope and a future."

BUILDING BLOCKS OF FAITH
Where He leads, He feeds.

Journal

Chapter Seven

At a little before 8 p.m. the plane descended from darkness and into the ambient glow of Nicaragua's capital city. When the aircraft reached the gate, the pilot turned off the air conditioning. A moist heat filled the cabin. Rich stood with the others, clutching his knapsack. He followed the conga-line crowd off the aircraft and up the concourse walkway, through an empty terminal and down a flight of steps to Customs and Immigration. He stood at the rear of the shortest line. When at last the official stamped his passport and welcomed him to Nicaragua, Rich walked toward a bank of floor-to-ceiling windows. An automatic door whooshed open as passengers exited. A pair of custodians unlimbered a buffing machine. Another stirred a bucket of wax. He wanted to remain inside, take a few more minutes to survey the scene beyond the doors, but a security officer hurried him along.

Rich walked out of the terminal and into the tropical night.

Across the street the marquee sign of a Best Western glowed bright. Cars honked, a bus sped past spewing diesel exhaust. He waited at a pedestrian crosswalk and then sprinted across four lanes of traffic.

Walking past the front desk and beyond a lounge area where a television barked at him in Spanish, he turned a corner and found the cyber-café. Locked. A sign showed guests how to swipe their room key to gain access. Rich returned to the lobby.

"Would it be possible for me to borrow one of your

computers to check my e-mail?"

"Are you staying in the motel?" the clerk asked.

"Not sure. Depends on what I find in my inbox."

"Only guests can access the Internet."

"Not even for just five minutes? I'm sort of in a bind. I was traveling with someone and he has my wallet. He missed our flight. I need to find out if he's coming at all."

"Sorry. Maybe you can charge the room to a credit card."

"That's the thing. I don't have my card with me. I won't be on long. You can watch me."

"I wish it were possible, *Señor*, but I'm the only one at the desk this evening."

"Is there a bank close by? Maybe I could call home and get someone to wire me some cash."

The clerk pointed out the front door. "About three kilometers that way there is a center. There you will find a bank. But I am sure it is closed."

"Not even for just a second? Maybe if I can e-mail my friend he can call and charge my room to his card."

The clerk shook his head.

"Can I just sit in the lobby for a moment? At least until I can figure something out?"

The clerk smiled. "But not too long."

Rich sank into the couch, the weight of fear swallowing him. Rummaging through his knapsack he found the guidebook. Once the woman had finally nudged him and said she was done, he'd been too tired to read. Now he fanned the pages, looking for a map of Managua. His eyes stopped when he came across a small envelope. On the front was his church's logo and address. A tithing envelope. He looked inside. There was the $112 Rich gave to the Pastor.

"How much for a room?" he asked, hurrying back to the desk clerk.

"$95 plus tax."

"Will this cover it?"

The clerk counted the money. "Yes. Just the one night?"

Rich was about to say yes but then paused. A moment earlier he'd been broke. Now he had enough money for a night's stay. But tomorrow, if the Pastor didn't arrive, he'd be in the same fix. He still needed a plane ticket home and he'd need to get to a bank for that. No way was he walking into the city, but if he spent all his money he couldn't pay for a taxi.

"How close is this place?" Rich asked, pointing to the map in his guidebook.

"Granada? Thirty, maybe forty kilometers."

"How would I get there? Tonight, I mean?"

"There is a bus that goes there, only…" The clerk looked at the clock. "The last one leaves at nine."

"Can I get there in time? The bus, I mean?"

Rich handed the clerk five dollars. "Would you find me a taxi that will take me to the bus terminal."

"This is not necessary, Señor," the clerk said, refusing the money.

Rich followed him outside. The clerk waved across the parking lot and the driver of a yellow Nissan pulled under the awning of the motel. The clerk went back inside.

"How much to take me to the bus terminal?" Rich asked.

The driver looked at the cash in Rich's hand and pointed to a twenty.

"Can you get me to the terminal before the bus leaves for Granada?"

"Si. I will get you there."

Sliding into the front seat of the car he clutched the knapsack to his chest. The safe thing to do was to remain in the hotel. But the safe thing would leave him stranded in a city he could not escape. No, the Pastor had told him on the ride to the airport that they were to meet a group in Granada and then drive down to San Juan Del Sur. If he could reach Granada this evening there was a chance he might hook up with the others. Then he'd deal with his money problems.

Twenty minutes later he arrived at the terminal. They pulled into the lot just as the bus driver stepped aboard. Rich, pointing to the map in his guidebook, asked, "Is this the bus to Granada?"

"Si, Granada."

"This bus, it will take me to Granada?"

"Si, si! Granada."

He stepped aboard and walked to the back, taking the last vacant seat. As he did, a young woman boarded. She stood on the steps, holding on to the safety bar as the bus bounced over the curb and turned into traffic. Standing, Rich pointed to his seat and took her place on the steps. Two blocks later the driver picked up another large group. Now the bus was so full the driver no longer bothered to close the door. They sped off into the night; the pavement became a blur. Only his grip on the safety bar kept him from tumbling out of the bus and under its tires.

They rolled through the city, picking up passengers, dropping off too few. Young Hispanic men drenched in sweat pressed against him. The bus bounced along rough pavement. A boom box blasted next to his ear. They passed a vacant field crowded with young boys playing soccer under the glare of headlights. The crowd on the bus swelled. He wished he'd kept his seat.

A half hour later they reached the center of the city. Passengers hopped off, most not waiting for the bus to come to a stop. The crowd thinned.

Rich took a seat near the window. Sliding his hand underneath the knapsack so as not to be seen, he eased the cash back into the church envelope. As he did he felt something square and stiff. A business card. On the back, written in the Pastor's small script, were these words. "Rich, wherever you are, God is *with* you and speaking *to* you. Remember, if you listen to God and obey His voice you will find yourself doing things you couldn't possibly do without His help."

But how do I listen? How do I know it's your voice and not my own, God?

He rested his head against the window. In time the light poles and street signs disappeared. With nothing left but time and his own fears, he returned to the prayer journal.

What I need now is protection, he thought. His eyes fell onto the words of the 23rd Psalm.

The Lord Is My Shepherd
Andrea Merrell

The LORD is my shepherd; I shall not want.
Psalm 23:1

THE LORD IS MY SHEPHERD. I will not lack any good thing because He will liberally supply and fill to the full, every need that I have. He will supply all my needs according to His riches in Glory by Christ Jesus. He will do exceedingly, abundantly above all I could ask or even imagine. All good and perfect gifts come down from the Father and He will even give me the desires of my heart as I trust and delight in Him.

THE LORD IS MY SHEPHERD. He causes me to lie down in, take refuge in, and be sustained by lush, green pastures, full of spiritual, emotional and physical nourishment. He goes before me and leads me beside cool, clean, still, sparkling waters of rest, refreshment and regeneration.

THE LORD IS MY SHEPHERD. He restores my soul. He fills me with the peace that passes all understanding. He washes me with the water of His Word and makes me clean within and without. He leads me in every right path. His Word is a lamp unto my feet and a light unto my path. He fills me with all Godly wisdom, knowledge and understanding. He sets me on a solid rock and a firm foundation.

THE LORD IS MY SHEPHERD. Even though I walk through valleys with shadows of death, evil and destruction, I will never be afraid; for He has not given me a spirit of fear, but of love, power and a sound mind. He has promised to never leave or forsake me and His perfect love in me casts out all fear. His rod and His staff will correct me, comfort me, protect me and keep me on a right path.

THE LORD IS MY SHEPHERD.   In the very midst of my enemies, He prepares a lavish banquet table with all manner of spiritual and physical sustenance. Whatever I need is there. He gives me all things that pertain to life and Godliness. He pours the anointed oil of gladness on my head and my cup runs over with His joy and with all the fullness of life.

THE LORD IS MY SHEPHERD.   Without a doubt, the mercy, goodness, blessings and favor of God will follow me each and every day that I live on this earth; then I will dwell in His great house, His Kingdom, the place He has prepared just for me, forever and ever, world without end.

THE LORD IS MY SHEPHERD.   What else could I possibly need?

***

PRAYER
Father, help me to trust, tithe and tell others of your faithfulness.

BUILDING BLOCKS OF FAITH
Do you examine God's word and obey, or do you examine your finances and do what you can afford?

_____

_____

_____

_____

_____

_____

_____

_____

_____

_____

_____

_____

_____

_____

_____

_____

_____

_____

_____

_____

_____

_____

_____

_____

_____

_____

A Lesson in Counting
Jan Loy

"Count it pure joy, my brothers, whenever you face trials
of many kinds, because you know that the testing of your
faith develops perseverance. Perseverance must finish its
work so that you may be mature and complete,
not lacking anything."
James 1:2-4

I was proud and smiling as I listened to my 2-year old grandson count from 1 to 10 perfectly! Of course, he is very smart, but I also recognized that the "counting lessons" from his mom and dad had taken root in him. They had captured teachable moments here and there, and the efforts paid off.

The Lord is just as diligent with me when it comes to counting lessons. He is teaching me to count the trials of life as "pure joy." This is not the standard way to respond in difficulties, so I have to set aside my normal way of thinking. How can I count something that is a problem as a joy? The task is not easy, but these gentle reminders help me as I learn to count His way:

- Each difficulty is an opportunity for me to grow.
- Each trial brings its own "gift."
- Each testing offers me a new perspective.

As with any lesson, learning to count the Lord's way takes some time and effort. But we have help from an excellent Teacher who is patient, understanding, and who loves us with His whole heart. So the next time difficulties come along—stop, take a deep breath and say, "Lord, I'm ready for my counting lesson!"

PRAYER
Lord, I'm ready for my counting lesson. Help me to
count it as pure joy when I face tough times.

BUILDING BLOCKS OF FAITH
Faith is a gift. It grows through use.

Journal

_____

_____

_____

_____

_____

_____

_____

_____

_____

_____

_____

_____

_____

_____

_____

_____

_____

_____

_____

Silent Wings
Danny Woodall

*"And so, from the day we heard, we have not ceased
to pray for you, asking that you may be filled with
the knowledge of his will in all spiritual wisdom and
understanding, so as to walk in a manner worthy of the
Lord, fully pleasing to him, bearing fruit in every good
work and increasing in the knowledge of God."*
Colossians 1:9-10

Five hours before the Allied troops hit the beaches of
Normandy, glider pilots flew troops and supplies behind
enemy lines. Gliders were towed by a cargo plane, and
flew at low altitude over the English Channel. Once
across the water, the pilots maneuvered the planes to
increase altitude and avoid hitting trees. After clearing
the trees, the gliders were cut loose to fly over the coastal
areas of France. Crossing the English Channel caused
many flights to be like a foggy roller coaster ride. After
an unusually rough landing, they placed supplies and
gave reinforcement to the men landing on the beaches.
The exploits of these brave men are included in The
Silent Wings Museum located near Lubbock, Texas.

For Christians, this world is like being behind
enemy lines. God has given us our own supply package;
it's called the Bible. The truths that are found within its
pages will provide strength to get us through the day.
They aren't spiritual facts for us to use in Bible Trivia,
but knowledge we can use to live in the manner worthy
of Christ.

In the book of James we find that we're to be *quick
to listen, slow to speak, and slow to anger.* When I have to
deal with problems at work it doesn't matter if I have a

quick come back or a smart answer. I should listen and rely on the Holy Spirit to help me act as I should, so those around me will see Christ.

Your daily Bible reading is not just a spiritual exercise routine, but a source of spiritual strength. Let the words of the Bible guide your life, and be a witness for Christ.

Like the Allied troops were able to advance because of the supplies planted by the glider pilots, we will gain strength from God's Word. In this way, we will advance the cause of Christ.

PRAYER
Father, help me go to You first. May I seek guidance through your Word and Spirit. Then help me be about the business of your kingdom.

BUILDING BLOCKS OF FAITH
The great miracles of the Bible required acts of obedience first. Study His word and be encouraged.

Journal

_____

_____

_____

_____

_____

_____

_____

_____

Where are You, Lord
Shelby Rawson

"By faith he left Egypt, not being afraid of the anger of the king, for he endured as seeing him who is invisible."
Hebrews 11:27

Where are you, Lord? I do not feel your presence. Tears streak familiar paths on lonely cheeks as I question the whereabouts of my Father. I know You must be near. My memory recalls your Word… It tells me that You won't leave me and that You love me with an everlasting love. Yet as I sit in this heart's turmoil, my unbelief is suffocating.

And, once again I am reminded of my feet. Feet that fail me. Feet that walk in fear. Feet that forget faith.

"I AM. I am here." Your voice echoes in my heart. "I have not called you to walk alone. I have called you to walk by faith. And I know you are afraid. Will you give me your fear? Will you wear My strength in your weakness?"

Can I give Him my fear? I am terrified to lay down the walls of my heart and move. To take the hand of God and move forward in faith is impossible while behind my illusion of safety . . . my suffocating familiarity . . . my walls. So, I must choose. Silent fear behind false security? Or faith in the hands of a loving Father who calls me to risk?

Here is the dilemma. My heart knows the cost involved with taking risks. Yet there is a price to pay in the absence of risk, as well. If I fixate on hurtful lessons from my past, then my present and future are like a kite tied to a chain—failing to fly. The kite may get lift if the wind (good experiences) is strong enough. Painful experiences should be like an anchored kite string—where God is the anchor. He knows we cannot forget the string tying us to our past. Yet, if we let Him hang on to it, the string is free to let the kite soar.

I don't want my life to be safely on the ground. I want to soar, though my fears would deny me flight. Therefore, by faith I will tie my string to the Father's hand and believe that He is able to direct this kite I believe to be so tattered. For when the Master holds the kite, He sees not the rips and stains of a paltry life, but the vibrant hues colored by the story He has written for my journey. When I quit struggling to control the string He gave me and by faith embrace the story He has written for this life, then I leave my fears in His invisible hand and take flight.

PRAYER
Lord, I don't want my life to be grounded in fear. I want to soar with Your Spirit. Help my life to take flight.

BUILDING BLOCKS OF FAITH
God wants to give us big visions, greater challenges and grand adventures for Him.

Journal

_____

_____

_____

_____

_____

_____

_____

_____

_____

Chapter Eight

Rich sat at the back of the bus alone. He'd been riding for almost an hour. Ahead, on the crest of a slight rise, lay a bank of gas lantern lights marking the outer limits of a city. The highway gave way to a cobblestone street littered with plastic cola bottles and paper wrappings, dead branches and clumps of soggy straw. A burrow pulling a cart waited for the bus to pass. They turned onto a block dwarfed by a three-story warehouse-like structure. Through the open doors of the second level a large boom dangled a bail of hay. The musty smell of burlap mingled with diesel fumes. At the end of the block, the bus pulled into a dirt lot and stopped. The driver stood and looked toward the rear of the bus.

"Granada."

"This is Granada?" Rich asked.

"Si, Granada."

Rich hugged his knapsack and stepped off. As he walked toward the sidewalk he heard the driver padlock the doors to the bus. Following the advice of the devotional, Rich turned toward the light and began to walk.

Ahead lay a tree-lined plaza. Beyond that an open shelter with a tin roof and vendor stalls. He passed a cemetery with enormous marble tombs. When he reached the plaza he felt the moist warmth of a lake breeze, smelled the sour odor of exposed mud flats and rotting fish. He walked up the steps of the Hotel Alhambra and through the landscaped patio garden to the front desk. He looked at the chalkboard displaying room rates. His heart fell. The Alhambra was more expensive than the Best Western.

He checked the time. A quarter past 10 p.m. Leaving the Best Western had been a mistake. There he had a safe room, if for only one night. Here he had nothing. No room, no friends, no clue what to do next. He walked back down the steps of the hotel and stood, looking back toward the bus parking lot. Maybe he could find a way to sneak back aboard.

"Room, Señor?"

The voice of the young man startled him.

"Dis place is muy carísimo," the teen said, cutting his eyes toward the ornate lobby of the Alhambra. "I find you a place, no?"

The boy started down the street without waiting. Rich followed. They turned at the corner and walked two blocks, moving away from the lights of the plaza. A left, another right and then three blocks more. Rich grew certain that the boy was about to rob him—or worse. He'd never hit a man, never used his fists at all. He wasn't sure how he'd react if the boy jumped him or even if it would matter. A young man like that out at night stalking gringos could only have one thing on his mind.

"My name is Dominic."

"You sure you're taking me to a motel?"

"Si. Only my belly. It hurts. I need some beans." He clutched his stomach as if in pain.

"Later. After you find me a place to sleep."

At the next intersection Dominic hesitated. *This is it. He'll try to take me here.* With one hand Rich held the strap of his knapsack, with the other he made a fist.

"Wait here." Dominic hurried down an alley,

ducking into a building.

Rich stood alone in the darkness. A scripture came to mind, one he'd read earlier on the bus. *"In times of trouble He shall hide me in His pavilion. He will hide me in the secure place of His tabernacle. He shall set me high upon a rock."*

A few minutes later Dominic returned. "Dat place is no good. Twenty dollars, American. I find you a better place. Only… my belly."

"Here." Rich reached into his knapsack and handed Dominic a Granola bar. "It's all I have."

"Gracias." He ripped off the wrapper and began to chew. "Dis way."

They started toward a city block anchored by a large cathedral. Atop the steeple in the faint light of darkness, Rich saw the cross pointing toward the stars. They passed the church and had almost reached the end of the block before Dominic stopped and knocked on a small door. Inside Rich heard the slow shuffling of feet, the sound of slippers on hard tile.

A short, round man with a gray beard opened the door aside and Dominic spoke to him in Spanish.

The man studied Rich. "You need a room?"

"Yes, but first I have to know how…"

"Ten dollars. You want to see it?"

Rich wondered if he should but, really, what did it matter. Anything was better than sleeping on the street. He reached into his front pocket but the German said, "You can pay in the morning. When we're open."

Rich felt in his pocket anyway. Opening the envelope he handed Dominic ten dollars. "For the beans."

"Gracias, Señor. Gracias."

After showering under a bare pipe and brushing his teeth, Rich returned to his room. A ceiling fan clicked as it spun, distributing the heat of stale air. The swayback springs of a rusty bed creaked as he sat on the edge of the mattress. His pillow smelled of hair gel but he'd never been so glad to have a bed in his life. He fell to his knees, clasped his hands together and, with tears welling up, he prayed, thanking God for guiding him to Granada, the young man and the room.

Exhausted, he fell onto the bed. He was about to turn off the light when he remembered the journal and began to read. Not out of fear this time, or desperation but out of gratitude. For the first time he began to believe that God was real. Really real. And that He really cared.

I Want New Flooring
Loree Lough

"The Lord maketh poor, and maketh rich:
he bringeth low, and lifteth up."
1 Samuel 2:7

The floors in my house are about as low they can get, and oh, what I wouldn't give to lift them all up . . . and toss them into the nearest dumpster!

Built in the early '70s, every room in my house reflected the styles of my least favorite decade. Picture a dull-black slate foyer, faded indoor-outdoor carpeting on the sun porch, scratched white kitchen tile, lackluster oak in the living room . . . connected with cheesy aluminum strips held in place by clunky screws that scrape the soles of my shoes, snag my socks, and draw blood when I'm barefooted.

Every time I see the *Lumber Liquidators* commercial on TV, I drool. The very sight of Brazilian cherry hardwood makes me sigh. One seamless material, flowing from room to room. I didn't get that giddy the first time I fell in love!

It won't surprise you that I recently asked my husband, "When the income tax refund gets here, how 'bout we spend it on new flooring?" Imagine my surprise when he said, "In this economy? Are you out of your ever-lovin' mind? There is absolutely nothing wrong with these floors!"

Sez you, I wanted to counter.

But I didn't, because ours has always been an old-fashioned marriage. He's the boss, especially when it comes to finances. He's the guy who pinched pennies until Lincoln cried, who held dollar bills so tightly

Washington winced. But the result is an itty bitty Rainy Day Fund that helps me sleep peacefully at night and, considering what he endured to make it possible, I don't have a problem with letting him make the money decisions.

God has always given my husband the confidence and common sense to lead our family wisely—to provide for us properly. I just had to learn to trust that his frugal ways would be best for us in the long run. And they were. His trust in God to provide adequately for his family has always been successful. They (God and my hubby) protect us like that.

So, I guess I'll just keep on imagining the day when I'll head for the coffeemaker in the early morning hours, a blissful smile on my face as I glide across an expanse of smooth new flooring that flows like a gleaming river from room to room.

Well, a girl can *dream* of walking on walnut . . . if she's walking with the Lord!

❧❧❧

PRAYER
Father I know what I have may not seem like much but, because all that I've received comes from you, I count my home as a part of your Kingdom. And you are welcome to stay anytime.

BUILDING BLOCKS OF FAITH
Satan controls us through our lust for money.

Journal

_____
_____
_____
_____
_____
_____
_____
_____
_____
_____
_____
_____
_____
_____
_____
_____
_____
_____
_____
_____
_____
_____
_____
_____
_____
_____
_____

Serving Numbers?
Jennifer Becker Landsberger

"No one can serve two masters. He will either hate one and love the other, or be devoted to one and despise the other. You cannot serve God and mammon."
Matthew 6:24

Every time I crawled into bed and closed my eyes, numbers raced through my head: $1,000 for the entertainment center; maybe we shouldn't have gotten it. I can't believe the new uniforms for my husband are going to cost $600. Gas is down, but milk is up. It seemed like I hadn't slept in days.

As I tossed and turned, I tried to pray. I say tried because I hadn't seen much success with that recently. As I prayed, calm descended over me for the first time in days. I remembered that Jesus had been born in a stable. I remembered Peter and Andrew dropped their nets and followed Jesus when called. They didn't stand there calculating how much they were losing by just dropping their nets and leaving the catch un-sold.

I know that money is required. Working and earning a paycheck are not intrinsically evil things. Going and buying groceries, clothes, or a DVD is not evil. However, when I waste all of my time worrying about money, I'm very close to worshipping something besides God. God should be the center of my life every day, all day. It is sometimes hard to trust. Yes, Christians do have financial troubles. Nowhere in the Bible does God promise we will have all of the material possessions we want and never have to think about money. In fact, it says the opposite–not to build up our treasure on earth and not to worship anything besides God.

No matter how dire the situation, God is not going

to let you starve to death. You may have to give up your pride and ask Him for help. You may have to ask others for help. But remember, above all, there is a reason for the troubles we go through; we simply have to trust that God knows what He is doing.

I offer you a challenge. Each time you have a thought about money, go pick up your Bible and read a verse. Let God guide your reading. Trust that He knows what is best.

PRAYER
Father, help me to trust in You, in all times and in all ways.

BUILDING BLOCKS OF FAITH
Satan uses our fear of financial insecurity to keep us from doing what God has called us to do.

Journal

_____

_____

_____

_____

_____

_____

_____

_____

_____

Slipping in Financial Mud
David Loy

"When I said 'My foot is slipping', your love, O Lord,
supported me. When anxiety was great within me,
your consolation brought joy to my soul."
Psalm 94:18-19

Over the past few months, it has become crystal-clear (both in my mind, and on paper) that placing my hope in money only leads to disappointment. After losing a significant percentage of our investments in the Fall of '08, my wife and I sensed that our financial "feet" were slipping.

Anxious thoughts, especially regarding financial issues, can devastate even the strongest of wills. Like many Christians, I struggle to give complete control of my finances to God. However, I recently realized that God provides a clear path for those that are facing financial struggles. The guidance came from the Psalms.

"When I said 'My foot is slipping', your love, O Lord, supported me. When anxiety was great within me, your consolation brought joy to my soul."

In studying the confession of the Psalmist, I realized that he acknowledged he had a problem. He was slipping, unable to control the situation around him. He could not solve the problem on his own. He spoke this problem to the Lord, and asked for help.

For me personally, consolation comes through reading scripture like this one, and remembering God's promises to provide for His people. God always provides the necessary support–through His Love and consolation. But first we must ask.

Placing hope and trust in money, financial security, retirement savings, etc. will never provide the pure joy that comes with completely trusting our Father to provide for our needs. Are your finances preventing you from experiencing real joy through God's provision? What do you need to change about your approach to money that will allow for God to have complete control?

PRAYER
When my foot is slipping, Lord, Your strong arm supports me. When my anxiety is great, your promises bring joy to my soul.

BUILDING BLOCKS OF FAITH
God loves aggressive faith, so whatever He's told you to do, go for it.

Journal

_____

_____

_____

_____

_____

_____

_____

_____

_____

_____

God's Faithfulness
Pat Jeanne Davis

*"All things work together for good to those
who love the Lord."*
Romans 8:28

My husband had a long commute five days a week
to our church. His work there was mentally exhausting,
but Joseph was happy. Then circumstances changed—
he lost his job. His disappointment was keen and his
spirit crushed. Joseph felt that God was displeased with
him. This became a nagging and recurring thought.

Joseph needed encouragement. My husband's
emotional and spiritual well being were more of a
concern than how we were going to manage financially.
I prayed for him and myself as I waited on the Lord for
direction. Then I began to see the hand of God in our
experience.

We discovered that, under the pension plan Joseph
was enrolled in, he could apply for early retirement
benefits. This was our first indication that God was
working on our behalf.

I've been a full time homemaker for fifteen years. I
decided to claim Social Security benefits this year at age
sixty-two. I learned our boys were eligible for children's
benefits as well. The Lord is faithful. He was providing
for us.

It was re-enrollment time once again. Would
we be able to continue to provide our sons with the
Christ-centered schooling? After applying for financial
assistance, we were given a 40% reduction on the
following year's tuition. We were overjoyed!

During these hard times, we learned how to live

more frugally. Fortunately, our home is mortgage free. But the high cost of utilities was another concern. I applied for financial help with those costs and received discounts on our electric and heating bills.

Since my husband's unemployment, the blessings have been many. Johnny and Tim only got to see their dad a short time each day when he worked full time at our church. Now he sees them off to school in the morning and picks them up later. Their dad now has the time to sit and talk with them. This is a witness to God's faithfulness to our family during a time of crisis.

We walk by faith and not by sight. It's during times of uncertainty that God reveals Himself. You too can experience God's faithfulness. Jesus promised that He will not leave nor forsake us. Look to Him in changed situations and see new mercies.

PRAYER
Lord, when I can't change the circumstances, change my heart.

BUILDING BLOCKS OF FAITH
True "social security" lies in the arms of Christ.

Journal

_____

_____

_____

_____

_____

_____

_____

Chapter Nine

Rich took a seat on the yellow bus. Outside his window, street vendors hawked bananas, mangos and live chickens. Wooden carts and portable tables ran along one side of the dirt parking lot that served as the bus terminal. Behind the stalls was a cinderblock wall about eight feet high. Spiked glass made from broken cola bottles gave the rim an emerald tint. The simplicity of the security seemed both impressive and necessary. In a country where poverty bred desperation, even rudimentary forms of protection offered a measure of comfort. How well he knew.

Less than an hour earlier he'd wakened to the sound of a shrill whistle just beyond the wall of his room. The unfamiliar room and stifling heat had made it hard to sleep. Only in the morning, while his German host poured him a cup of coffee, had Rich learned that the whistle meant police were chasing away a vandal, thief or worse. When he thought of how close he'd come to sleeping on a bench in the public park, he thanked God again for the security of a bed.

After his shower he logged on to the Internet to check his e-mail. At first the configuration of the keyboard confused him, but he adjusted and managed to pull up his account. Sorting through the messages, he finally found one from his Pastor. His mission team had checked out the day before. Apparently his flight had been listed as "cancelled" on the arrival board.

"They'll be at the Hotel Casa Blanco in San Juan Del Sur until Tuesday," the Pastor's e-mail said. "Then they're traveling up to the coast to Tola."

Hurrying back to his room, Rich grabbed the guidebook and studied the map of Nicaragua's Pacific coast. San Juan Del Sur lay just north of the Costa Rican border and a long way from Granada. He'd shown the map to his host.

The German explained that a bus ran from Granada to Rivas. "From there you can take a taxi to the coast. But you should hurry. The seats fill fast."

He'd skipped breakfast and returned to the dirt lot where his bus had parked the night before. Now he sat eight rows back from the driver's seat. Atop the bus was a large metal basket filled with vegetables, paper goods, building supplies and at least one bike. He'd been sitting a long time. Apparently the scheduled departure times were like airline schedules and more of a suggestion than certainty. The driver remained outside chatting with an old woman in a polka dot dress selling mangos from a large basket resting on the ground beside her bare feet.

Finally the bus began to fill. Passengers stood chest-to-back in the aisle. A small fan over the empty driver's seat whirred. A popular song blasted from the radio, bringing back memories of Peg and the time the two of them drove all night to the beach for no reason. That was the last time she'd seen the ocean.

Three weeks later they wheeled her into surgery. She never came out.

Rich wondered now if the words of Phil Collins were meant to be prophetic. Perhaps God was speaking to him in the same way that small voice had spoken to him the night they'd driven to the coast. "She needs this," he'd found himself thinking that evening. "She needs to see the vastness of the ocean and feel the warmth of the sun on her face."

The driver climbed aboard and started the engine.

Rich rested his head against the edge of the window frame, inhaling diesel fumes. He tried not to dwell on the fact that he was in a third-world country at a little past eight on a Monday morning in December when he should be in his office.

He hummed along, straining to hear the singer's words over the chatter of passengers. "She calls out to the man on the street. 'Sir, can you help me? It's cold and I've nowhere to sleep. Is there somewhere you can tell me?'"

Hadn't that been him last night, desperate for a place to lay his head? And hadn't Peg complained of the cold as she lay in the hospital bed, even after he'd tucked the blanket wrapped around her?

"He walks on, doesn't look back, he pretends he can't hear her. He starts to whistle as he crosses the street, seems embarrassed to be there."

Was he embarrassed to be on this bus among these people? Did he really think his money made him better than them?"

"Oh, think twice. It's just another day for you and me in paradise."

Granada wasn't paradise. Not even close. It was dirty, hot and rife with crime. And yet, these were God's people, too. He remembered how Peg talked of living in paradise with God. Was she there, now? Had her faith carried her to a place of peace? How could he know? How could he be sure?

The song ended; the bus pulled away. As they navigated the narrow roads of Granada, he realized that for him it was just another day in paradise. Not a day of prosperity, perhaps, but beauty nonetheless. He sensed God calling him to something new, a pilgrimage that was more than just a mission trip. He was out of his element, way beyond his comfort zone. But then hadn't Christ left the splendor of His Father's kingdom to travel to an impoverished people? For Jesus, leaving the luxury of His palace to save and serve mankind was more than a minor inconvenience. It was His life's mission. It had, in fact, cost Him his life.

The bus accelerated when it reached the outskirts of town. They passed a cemetery and a billboard sign that advertised canopy tours in a rain forest over Volcán Mombacho. Thankful for a safe night's rest and to be on the bus heading to the coast, he opened the old journal once more. Perhaps he'd find comfort in the words of others who'd already traveled the road of faith. The paraphrased words of the writer stunned him.

"If we are faithful with our money, Jesus says we'll be entrusted with spiritual riches. Luke 16:11."

Beneath that passage was the story of a woman who'd given away the proceeds from a yard sale to help the poor, the recounting of an Old Testament tale about an impoverished widow giving away her last meal, and a man who'd emptied his wallet to help another. Like the writers in the journal, Rich had seen the need of those living in squalor. Was he a self-made success? Or had his wealth come because he'd been fortunate to be born in a country that allowed for him to succeed? Had he become so addicted to the palatial comforts of his home that he couldn't share his wealth with others?

But I'm just one man, he thought, watching as the lush vegetation became a blur outside his window. *How much of a difference can I make in these people's lives?*

He closed the journal, refusing to read further. Then he thought of the money in his billfold, the tithe he'd given to the Pastor. Technically, *none* of the cash was his. *All* the money had been provided to him by others. He was spending someone else's money; even *he* could admit that. A voice, maybe his own, whispered to him. "Trust me, not the methods."

With a heavy sigh he turned the page and began to read. If he was going to live by faith and do what he knew had to be done, he'd need the encouragement and reassurance of others. What would come next would be the toughest test yet.

Empty Jars
Eddie Jones

*Elisha said, 'Go around and ask all your neighbors
for empty jars. Don't ask for just a few.'"*
II Kings 4: 3

Her husband had been a Godly man who revered the Lord. As a couple, they'd served in the temple, tithed and offered prayers for the sick and lame. But now her husband was dead and the creditors were calling, threatening to take her boys. Abandoned and scared, she turned to the man of God.

"How can I help you?" asked Elisha. *"Tell me, what do you have in your house?"* Her response was like so many of us who have lost jobs, health coverage, savings, and faith in our future. *"Nothing,"* she replied. *"Just a little olive oil."*

"Go around and ask all your neighbors for empty jars," he said. *"Don't ask for just a few."*

Empty jars? That was his advice? He wanted her to ask for jars, not oil, money or food? Why? To remind her of her loss? So the neighbors could see her beg? To shame her to tears?

The rules for economic success have changed for our generation, but have we? The fundamentals are broken, our faith in the system failing. The old ways aren't working—we aren't working. As unemployment rises, the stock market tumbles. What's left but fear?

"She left him and shut the door behind her... Her sons brought the jars to her and she kept pouring. When all the jars were full, she said to her son, 'Bring me another one.' But he replied, 'There is not a jar left.' Then the oil stopped flowing."

"Now, sell the oil and pay your debts," said Elisha. *"You and your sons can live on what is left."*

I don't know what financial crisis has rocked your world but I know this. God has made us stewards of His truth, and our time and talents. He has commanded us to use our lives for His glory. To do so requires faith, not in a system... but in a God who loves not only the widow and orphan, but the unemployed and bankrupt.

God's grace is limitless but our ability to receive it is not. He calls us to gather empty jars in preparation for his blessing of abundance.

What you already have may seem like nothing, but God asks you to give, so take inventory of your skills, talents, resources and assets. Gather your jars, pots and kettles and pour yourself into His work. Who knows but that He wants to fill your cupboard with a miracle?

PRAYER
Father, what I have is enough. May my small faith be at work when I have no other resource but You.

BUILDING BLOCKS OF FAITH
What you have may not seem like much but if God asks for it, then it's priceless.

Journal

Sam I Am
Irene Brand

*"But when you give to the needy, do not let your left hand
know what your right hand is doing, so that your
giving may be in secret. Then your father, who sees
what is done in secret, will reward you."*
Matthew 6: 3-4

I've been the treasurer of our local church for many years. It's one of my self-made rules that I never reveal personal contributions of our members. If they want someone to know what they give to the work of the Lord, they reveal it; I don't.

However, we have a couple in our church who are among the most generous, unselfish people I know. Since most of the things I've witnessed have been incidents of the husband's, I will refer to the man. Although this is not his name, for privacy reasons, I'll call him Sam.

Sam is not an educated man, but he worked hard all of his life and received good compensation during most of those years. He and his wife have a comfortable home and they drive serviceable vehicles, but they do not live in luxury. It's quite likely that they don't have a large nest egg laid away for their declining years, for they aren't interested in accumulating possessions.

Sam never passes a man begging on the street corner without giving him money. A young couple in our church had to take their child to a distant city for medical treatment. The wife told me that they had no expense money, but Sam slipped a hundred-dollar-bill in her pocket before they left.

A woman came during one of our evening church services asking for financial help. Our church designates a certain amount of money, which I, as treasurer, can give in such circumstances without further authorization. Sam and I talked with the woman. She said that what the church was giving wouldn't be enough. Sam gave the woman $40.00, all of the money he had in his billfold. She promised that she would return the money the next day. She didn't, but that didn't stifle Sam's giving spirit.

It's easy for us as Christians to give our tithe to God's work and think that we merit a pat on the back, but Sam's example reveals the New Testament policy of giving. We can more closely measure the depth of our giving when we consider how much we keep for ourselves.

❧

PRAYER
Father, help us to remember that what we give to others, we are really giving to You.

BUILDING BLOCKS OF FAITH
Faith requires that we do the possible and let God do the impossible.

Journal

_____

_____

_____

_____

_____

_____

_____

_____

Giving God Away
Kelli Regan

*"Each man should give what he has decided in his heart
to give, not reluctantly or under compulsion, for God
loves a cheerful giver. And God is able to make all grace
abound to you, so that in all things at all times, having
all that you need, you will abound in every good work."*
2 Corinthians 9:7-8

"Whoa!" Our accountant cautioned as he reviewed our tax return data. "Your charitable giving number is really high. It could raise a red flag." Instead of panicking my husband and I praised God.

See, years ago, giving to us meant tossing a spare twenty into the collection plate. The concept of tithing offended me—it seemed like a clever scheme to puff up the church coffers. Besides, how could we give away ten percent of our income when we couldn't even pay off our credit cards?

Then about six years ago I invited Jesus into my heart. As my faith grew and I experienced God's truth, I realized my attitude toward giving didn't line up with scripture.

As Paul explains, if we give little we'll receive little. Even if we give a lot, but do it with the wrong attitude, we don't please God. Because God's not after our money, He's after our hearts. Giving isn't a financial transaction, it's a spiritual one.

When my husband and I began to view giving from a biblical perspective, we slowly eased our grip on our finances. First, we set a reasonable giving goal, aiming for eventual tithing. Then we started chipping away at our credit card debt.

It was a slow, steady journey, but this past year the Spirit urged us to bridge our tithing gap and go straight to ten percent. On paper it seemed impossible, but we followed obediently.

A few months after we made this commitment, the economy imploded. Oddly, we never considered putting our giving on hold. Instead, we continued honoring our tithe as the first "bill" we paid each month. We also finished paying off our credit cards. Sure we've had to make sacrifices, but at a time when many are wringing their hands about their finances, we've experienced more freedom and peace than we've ever known.

Are you sharing your wealth as an act of love for Christ and His Church? If you're not sure about tithing, read Malachi 3:8-10. Does the thought of giving ten percent overwhelm you? Set a more comfortable goal and work toward a tithe. It's your attitude, not the amount, that matters most. Be patient and trust God.

Our best financial plans are worthless compared to the eternal security we have in Jesus.

PRAYER
Lord, you promised that I'll never go hungry or beg for bread. Help me to make sure others do not, as well.

BUILDING BLOCKS OF FAITH
God judges all our actions by our motives.

Journal

_____

_____

_____

_____

_____

_____

_____

_____

_____

_____

_____

_____

_____

_____

_____

_____

_____

_____

_____

_____

_____

_____

_____

_____

_____

_____

_____

Pay Back Time
Cindy Sproles

"Boaz replied, "I've been told all about what you have done…May the LORD repay you for what you have done. May you be richly rewarded by the LORD, the God of Israel, under whose wings you have come to take refuge."
Ruth 2:12

I love to give. Always have. It's a family trait that was passed from my grandmother to my mom who then gave it to me. My parents taught me to search for the good qualities of folks then latch hold and stroke those gifts. Encourage them. Provide simple needs if I could. Give whenever possible.

Through the years, seeking the good in others and giving encouragement has become second nature. I never know if my words make an impact but then, they weren't said for my benefit. They were done because there was a need that should be met and God said, "Cindy, you can do this." So I did.

There were times when giving someone a pat on the back was hard, especially when my words were tossed aside as unnecessary or worse—irrelevant. Still, it was the right thing, so I lifted them up with prayers and praise. Even when I saw my efforts squandered, the giving was never greater than the blessing of the gift.

I've received my share of compliments, too. God has provided kind words for me to glean just as He did for Ruth. But for me, receiving praise is harder than handing it out. I often don't feel worthy.

Recently, I was presented with a unique opportunity, a chance to use my gifts and passion for something I truly love. The project would open doors for our ministry and provide abundantly for my family. As I found myself trying to bring along my friend, he repeated over and over, "No, this is for you from God. This is repayment for what you've done for others. It's your time to glean." And I wondered, repayment for what? I simply don't think in those terms.

Ruth turned down a chance to return to her people in order to remain with a mother-in-law to whom she had no obligation. So when Ruth was rewarded for her kindness and loyalty, she had to be told to return, accept the kindness of Boaz and see it as a gift.

Who knows if this opportunity will prosper or fail? Only God knows. But I have learned no matter what we receive in return, just knowing that we've helped and blessed others is reward enough.

When God provides a field, glean. Accept His generosity from the hands of others. Say "thank you." That, too, is a way of showing His love to others. I'm grateful my mother taught me to give without question and I'm touched when God deems me fit for repayment. I still have a hard time accepting, but I'm learning.

Thanks Mom, for the lessons in giving. I love you.

PRAYER
Father thank you for our earthly families and heavenly help.

BUILDING BLOCKS OF FAITH
Provision is available in every situation if the people of God will obey His voice.

Journal

_____

_____

_____

_____

_____

_____

_____

_____

_____

_____

_____

_____

_____

_____

_____

_____

_____

_____

_____

_____

_____

_____

_____

_____

_____

_____

_____

_____

_____

_____

God's Yard on my Lawn
Kristi Buttles

"Everything under heaven belongs to me."
Job 41:11

"Hold a yard sale and donate the profits to the benevolence fund!"

Those words nearly knocked me off my chair. Our Pastor had challenged our church in a unique way because he understood that, while many of us didn't have extra money to give, we could donate the profits of a yard sale to help families with desperate needs in this difficult economy. Unknowingly, my husband, Bruce, and I had decided that week to hold a garage sale to fund a few home repairs and improvements.

My heart struggled over whether to keep or donate the profits. "How is it wrong to use this money to meet our own needs?" I asked myself. I told God I didn't understand why we shouldn't keep the money. He replied, "You have forgotten that none of it was yours to begin with. I own it all, and will do with it according to my plan." Somehow, I'd forgotten that the things we had to sell were given to us by God in the first place. They were not ours, nor were the profits from our yard sale.

Still, I struggled. Bruce and I talked about it again. "Yes, we need it," he said, "but, God is obviously saying there is another family who needs it more."

During our conversation, God reminded me of the talent parable in Matthew. We could keep our one talent (the garage sale profits) and it would be a drop of relief in our own bucket. Or, we could obey God and invest in His kingdom, trusting that He would meet our needs and those of the other families. After giving it more thought,

I realized that some of the needs we had were actually wants.

Thinking back to previous times, I thought I had given sacrificially when, in fact, I gave out of abundance. Sacrificial giving is exactly what Jesus did for us, and we are indebted to Him because of it. That week, we joyfully sacrificed the profits from our sale. In return, God met our true needs.

How much should believers give to others when we need it now or may need it soon? How can we be sure that God will meet our own needs? Can we trust Him to care for us?

As someone once told me, you can't out-give God. What will you give in His name today?

PRAYER
Lord, give me neither poverty nor riches, but only my daily bread. Otherwise I may have too much and disown you or become poor and steal.

BUILDING BLOCKS OF FAITH
The antidote to envy is becoming convinced of God's goodness.

Journal

_____

_____

_____

_____

_____

_____

_____

Chapter Ten

The white Toyota taxi pulled to the curb in front of a two-story motel in San Juan Del Sur. Rich handed the driver a twenty and told him to keep the change.

He stepped from the car and stood on the chipped fragments of what had once been a sidewalk. The taxi sped away; he walked across the street to a café overlooking a crescent-shaped beach. Out in the water fishing boats lay anchored, their hulls rocking gently to the swells working their way into the bay. Rich took a seat in the corner of the patio and set his knapsack on the empty chair beside him. Bamboo beams covered in palm sheaths provided shade from the afternoon sun. A ceiling fan distributed the smells of strong coffee and fried fish.

Rich ordered bottled water and then asked the location of the Hotel Casa Blanca. The waiter pointed down the block toward a two-story building. He paid for the water and hurried across the road to meet his group.

On the front porch a young couple in teal scrubs sat in rockers. Maybe they were part of his group. Rich walked through an open-air courtyard and into the lobby. He asked about his mission team.

"Lo siento, Señor. Dis morning, they leave."

"They left? Did they say if they were coming back?"

He shrugged. " I give you the same rate, no? Seventy. American."

That would take the rest of his money. A sense of

helplessness swept over him.

He'd abandoned his clients and flown to Central America so he could help a team of strangers he'd never met build a church in a village he couldn't even find in his guidebook. He'd nearly fallen from a speeding bus in Managua, narrowly missed getting mugged in Granada, and spent a night alone in a hostel infested with cockroaches. He'd spent too much money on taxi fares and bus tickets and he was no closer to meeting his group than he was when he left Washington. He should have never left the airport in Managua, never boarded the plane in the first place. He should've ignored his Pastor and stayed home to watch the Skins play the Packers in the snow. At least professional football was something he understood.

"The room, Señor."

"Maybe later. First I have to do something."

He returned to the café across the street. He sat for a long time watching a group of boys kick a soccer ball up and down the beach. Shirts and shoes formed the corners of make-believe goals. Make believe. That's all this trip was. A journey into fantasyland faith. How could he be so stupid? This was worse than getting bilked by shady hedge fund managers.

A gull came winging in high above the water. It circled once before diving into the water. When it took flight again, he saw the silver tail of a small fish trying to break free of the bird's beak. *Just like me,* he thought. *Trapped.*

"What do you want from me, God? I'm stuck; do you hear me? Stuck." His words were barely audible over the surge of surf rushing up the beach. "Don't you care?"

Silence.

He squinted against the glare of the sun reflecting off the water and closed his eyes.

"I have nowhere else to turn. You're it. I thought I was doing what you wanted me to do. It certainly wasn't what *I* wanted to do. Only a fool would have gotten on that plane the way I did. But I thought, you know, just once, I'd take a chance on you. Look what it got me."

Silence.

"About what I figured. Fantasyland faith. That's all this is."

He opened the journal for the final time, feeling not hope, but bitterness.

The Promise of Provision
Dr. Chris Stocklin

And my God will meet all your needs according to his glorious riches in Christ Jesus.
Philippians 4:19

Tears streamed down the man's face. "Dr. Stocklin, you're looking at a 75 year-old man who has nothing because I've spent everything." Even now, recalling his words, my heart aches for him.

The financial plight this man faced was because of his age and the inability to earn an income in order to reverse his unfortunate financial concerns. I think often about his words, "I have nothing because I've spent everything."

The lifestyle Jesus called His followers to abide was simple. Christ tells us a believer should be content with food, clothing, housing and drink. However, the simple lifestyle Jesus desired for His followers counters our current culture which fuels our greed.

Our nation endorses a consumer based economy which can now be defined as a consumer-credit based economy. The popular mantra of today, in order for the nation to experience a healthy, vibrant economy, is for the American consumer to buy, buy, buy, and spend, spend, spend! And we buy and spend whether we have the money or not.

Credit usage has reached record highs. In our world of convenience, where everyone wants a cell phone, a computer and a 52-inch television, I wonder how we ever managed without such amenities.

The Apostle Paul declared that God would meet our needs—needs being defined by the Holy scripture—not what current society, retailers or mass marketers would determine. Our economy is built upon spending and self-gratification, not saving... reckless decisions that lead to financial folly. Our daily choices *do* impact our future security, both in this life and the life to come.

The promise of scripture is that God will meet our needs. What is required of us? Faith. Faith in His promise. Faith in His faithfulness. Faith in our future in His hands.

If you are facing financial concerns, ask yourself these questions; "Can I afford it? Do I need it? Would God approve?" He will meet our needs, yes, but first we must seek Him, His will and His righteousness.

❧❧❧

PRAYER
Lord, you have promised to meet all our needs according to the glorious riches in Christ Jesus. May I trust you with my financial future.

BUILDING BLOCKS OF FAITH
Keep current with your debts, then set your financial goals based on God's leading.

Journal

_____

_____

_____

_____

_____

_____

_____

Provision Today, Tomorrow and Forever

Miralee Ferrell

"Who of you by worrying can add a single hour to his life?"
Matthew 6:27-29

One evening I slipped away to get alone with the Lord. We'd hit bottom and money was tight. Months earlier we'd listed our house for sale but there had been few showings and no offers. Sleepless nights plagued us both and the bills piled up. Something needed to change, but only the Lord could bring a buyer for our house. I had believed God's promise that He would care for our needs.

So why hadn't anything changed? I finished praying, struggling to quiet my emotions, seeking a measure of reassurance.

As I rested with eyes closed, knees bent, a peace filled my heart. I sensed a small voice whispering, "One week."

I stood and asked. "What does that mean?"

The answer nudged my heart. "Our house will sell in one week."

I wondered if I'd heard properly. We didn't even have any showings scheduled.

Two days later a friend called. Their relatives were flying up and wanted to see the house. When the couple arrived they spent two hours checking out the property. They returned the following day and made a substantial offer. Two days later, they signed papers and put down earnest money. The house sold in under one week.

Repeating the all-too-familiar words of Matthew six seems easy until a crisis hits. We often quote scriptures that promise provision but when our needs grow, it's hard to focus on the Lord. Fear sinks its talons in our minds and makes our hearts less receptive to God's word. But His word isn't applicable only if we *feel* that it's true. God's word is true all the time, regardless of our screaming emotions.

We can't always decipher how God works, but we can trust and obey. It didn't make sense that He could sell our house in one week, but I had a choice. Trust and praise Him for His promise and provision, or scoff at His words and the Spirit's nudging, and continue to live in doubt and fear. I chose to praise and believe.

God is the same yesterday, today and forever, and His provision isn't dependent on the economy or the housing market. He has His own kingdom community and it's far greater than anything we can imagine and He wants us to move in. If only we'll believe.

PRAYER
Father, help me to remember that the miracle comes after the mess, that my obedience often precedes your blessing.

BUILDING BLOCKS OF FAITH
God's ways are not our ways but they always work anyway.

Journal

_____

_____

_____

_____

_____

_____

_____

_____

_____

_____

_____

_____

_____

_____

_____

_____

_____

_____

_____

_____

_____

_____

_____

_____

_____

_____

_____

The Check's in the Mail
Andrea Merrell

"Give to others, and God will give to you. Indeed, you
will receive a full measure, a generous helping, poured
into your hand— all that you can hold."
Luke 6:38

God never ceases to amaze me with the creative ways He chooses to bless His children. I haven't found any money in a fish's mouth lately, or caught any pennies raining from Heaven, but every single time I reach the proverbial end of the rope, He comes through in surprising and unusual ways.

Just when the bills pile high and my checking account looks empty, provision seems to suddenly appear. It might be in the form of a rebate, refund or dividend check. Maybe it's a gift, bank error in my favor (yes, it really does happen), or receiving an unknown and unexpected inheritance. I've even had a couple of debts paid off or cancelled (honestly!) and wiped out completely. How and by whom I will probably never know.

What I do know is this: God is our source. He is our provider and has an abundant supply of whatever we need. When we become wise and obedient stewards with what He gives us and pray according to His Word, we can be sure He hears us. We can also trust in His faithfulness and rest in the fact that He will liberally supply.

If you're a giver, you know how we are to operate— *give and it shall be given.* The Word tells us to sow our seed in order to reap a harvest. When we *lay up treasure in Heaven* and make regular deposits into our Heavenly bank account, we can be confident that our funds are well protected, drawing interest, and available whenever we need them.

I can say without hesitation, God has never failed to meet my needs. The answer may not come when I think it should, or the way I anticipate, but it always comes, and it usually far exceeds my expectations.

Do you have a need today? Present it to God. Ask in faith, believing that you receive. Then, you can confidently say, "The check's in the mail."

PRAYER
Lord, may I never forget how you have provided for me over and over again in countless, creative, and unexpected ways. Thank you for your faithfulness.

BUILDING BLOCKS OF FAITH
Give generously, trust completely, and expect God to meet your needs, just as He promised.

Journal

God is My Stimulus Package
DiAnn Mills

"Trust in the Lord with all your heart and lean not on your own understanding. In all your ways acknowledge Him, and He will make your paths straight."
Proverbs 3:5-6

I remember the bleak day I realized I had enough food for two more days. I had no money and no job. How would I take care of my four young sons? I tried to pray, but fear hung suspended in my mind and choked any semblance of words. I wanted to cry, but realized that once I started, the tears might never end. Single parenting and children who had more needs than I could fill, paralyzed my thoughts.

Swallowing my pride, I phoned my parents in another state. Perhaps they'd take the boys until I got on my feet. The thought of parting with them made me physically ill. They had already dealt with abandonment issues from their father's recent departure, and I knew being separated from me would increase their insecurities – and mine.

After the phone call and the news that they felt something good would happen soon, I painted a smile on my face and went through the motions of preparing the boys' dinner. The doorbell rang, interrupting my silent prayer for faith. A middle-aged woman stood there, looking somewhat perplexed and nervous.

"Can I help you?" My voice released staggering emotions.

She nodded and gave me a faint smile. "I think so. God told me that the family living here needs food. I have my station wagon full of groceries."

My boys rushed to her vehicle and helped carry in bag after bag. Not since Christmas had they been so excited. Me either, for that matter.

God had sent an angel to feed my family! The food in those grocery bags fed us for a long time. Every item was something I would have purchased, even special treats. This blessing marked the beginning of many. Within a week I found a job directing a day care center, and my children never went hungry or without care. The true treasure was the provision of our faithful Father who ensured that our family never had to be separated.

PRAYER

Father, may I never be half-hearted in Your work. Help me to do what you have told me to do with all my might.

BUILDING BLOCKS OF FAITH

When we step out in faith, we see God's hand at work in dramatic acts of provision.

Journal

Mama, is it free?
Susan Dollyhigh

"The Spirit and the bride say, "Come!" And let him who hears
say, "Come!" Whoever is thirsty, let him come; and whoever
wishes, let him take the free gift of the water of life."
Revelation 22:17

Excitement was in the air as we gathered for Bible study at the homeless shelter.

"I'm being baptized next Sunday night. Will you come?" Jane asked. Jane had accepted Christ as her Savior the previous week at the shelter.

Kristen, a 12-year-old resident, then exclaimed, "I learned all about Jesus in Bible school and I want to be baptized too."

Turning to her mother, Kristen asked, "Mama, can I? Can I be baptized?"

"You don't need to be baptized now," Mama responded.

A hush fell over the small group as Kristen's chin quickly dropped to her chest. Even as my heart ached for Kristen, we began our lesson which interestingly enough was on the plan of salvation. We talked about how God loved the world so much that he gave his only Son so that whoever believes in Him could have eternal life. We talked about Jesus being the way, the truth and the life and the only way to the Father.

As we talked, the little girl continued to plead her case. "I know that. I learned that in Bible school. Mama, why can't I be baptized?"

"Hush. We'll talk about it some other time," Mama said.

"Mama, I need to do this. Please?" the little girl begged.

"I said 'No,'" came Mama's reply.

And then the child who had been told "no" so

many times because the things she wanted in life cost too much asked, "Well, Mama is it free?"

Silence once again fell over the group. Even Mama didn't have a quick answer to that question. Kristen's eyes then turned to me and the answer that sprang from my heart was, "Yes, baby girl, it is free. It is God's gift to us and is free to all."

The following Sunday evening the baptism of those two was a glorious affair to behold. And even though Mama didn't attend, a radiant-faced little girl stood in the baptismal waters as she announced that she had accepted the one thing in life that is truly free, the gift of Jesus Christ as her Savior.

Even in the worst of economic times when we may be concerned about the cost of even our most basic needs, we can rest assured that the cost of our greatest need truly is free to us all.

PRAYER

Father, thank you that as we trust in You for our daily provisions, You provide. Thank You that when we accept Jesus as our Savior, You freely provide the gift of eternal life.

BUILDING BLOCKS OF FAITH

Fine wine comes from smashed grapes and no one saves the squished skins. Drink in the Spirit of Christ and be set free.

Faith & FINANCES

Journal

_____

_____

_____

_____

_____

_____

_____

_____

_____

_____

_____

_____

_____

_____

_____

_____

_____

_____

_____

_____

_____

_____

_____

_____

_____

_____

_____

The Blessing of the Lord
Virginia Smith

*"...the Lord blessed the household of the Egyptian because of
Joseph. The blessing of the Lord was on everything
Potiphar had, both in the house and in the field."*
Genesis 39:3

We all like to feel that we're making a difference.
For many years I was employed by the headquarters
of a seafood restaurant chain. Though I enjoyed my
job, at times it was difficult to see that my efforts had
any lasting effect. I mean, I didn't have a significant
impact on people's lives, as those who work in the
medical profession do. Nor was I feeding their souls as a
minister would. No, if I worked my hardest and focused
on striving for absolute excellence in my job, the best I
would do is sell more fish and increase my company's
stock price. Where's the lasting value in that?

Surely Joseph must have had similar thoughts. There
he was, betrayed by his own brothers, then bought by a
wealthy Egyptian to be a house slave. He, who was his
father's favorite and one of God's chosen people, was
working as a lowly servant for a foreigner. How much
more futile could life get? Why strive for excellence
when the results of your hard work would only mean
success for someone who didn't even know the Lord?

But Joseph didn't look at it that way. He knew God
was with him regardless of where he worked. He was
one of the Lord's chosen, and God blessed his service to
his Egyptian master. Joseph proved his trustworthiness,
and the Lord not only showered Potiphar's household
with success, He also promoted Joseph to positions of
increasing prominence, and blessed him with enough

riches and food to eventually save his people from starvation.

I serve the same Lord as Joseph. He stands ready to bless my efforts with success, even though the work I do might seem trivial in the grand scheme of things. But it's not trivial to God. I'm His child, His chosen instrument to demonstrate trustworthiness and integrity in whatever situation He places me. The result? Blessings for my employer, and for me.

Besides, in these uncertain times, there's nothing wrong with a strong stock price!

***

PRAYER
Lord, bless my efforts with success, even when the work I do seems trivial.

BUILDING BLOCKS OF FAITH
Take "stock" of your blessings, then give thanks.

Journal

_____

_____

_____

_____

_____

_____

_____

_____

_____

What to Do in a Drought
Tina Givens

"And it came to pass after a while, that the brook dried up, because there had been no rain in the land."
I Kings 17:7

My resources were evaporating and it seemed like the job market had completely dried up.

Two years ago I found myself unemployed for nine months and experiencing tremendous financial pressure. I trusted God, but there were moments when I felt drained and helpless.

Little did I know that God was about to unlatch the floodgates of heaven. After months of rejection, I received an unsolicited phone call from a past employer. We'd lost touch over the years, but he'd tracked me down through a mutual friend and called to offer me a job. That is, 'if I was interested'. If I was interested? It was all I could do, not to run outside and turn cartwheels in the street!

As difficult as it was, I kept my eyes focused on the promises of God. He would provide for me in His own time. The Lord was faithful and His timing perfect. A little while longer and I would have been in financial ruin.

The brook providing drinking water for the prophet Elijah dried up because of drought. But God miraculously provided another source. When finances are tight for me, I wonder what Elijah must have thought as he watched the water dry up. Did he worry in his crisis like I sometimes do? Or did he have confident trust that the Lord would provide?

What about you? Perhaps your brook has dried up

and you are in need. Maybe you are alternating between fear and faith as you watch the forecast and see a zero percent chance of rain.

God has not forgotten you. His plan provides in spite of how helpless you feel or how hopeless the situation looks. Keep praying. Remember the countless examples in the Bible and in your life of the Lord's faithfulness. Dwell on them and build your faith.

God will sustain you during the dry times and, in His perfect timing, He will send the rain.

PRAYER
You are my God for ever and ever. Guide me to the very end.

BUILDING BLOCKS OF FAITH
Faith is believing something will happen before it does.

Journal

Don't Flinch
David Stearman

"For God is not a man that He should lie, neither is He a son of man that he should change His mind. Has he spoken, and will He not do it, or has He promised and will He not make it good?"
Numbers 23:19

I grew up as a country boy, learning to shoot a rifle at an early age. Outdoor sports, when introduced appropriately and responsibly, have the potential of teaching important life-lessons to kids. One such lesson I'd call "Avoiding the Flinch."

A high-powered rifle makes a loud noise, accompanied by a sharp nudge to the shoulder referred to as a "kick." This combination of crack and push tempt the marksman to flinch just before pulling the trigger, thus drawing him off target. If the marksman takes his focus off of his mark at just the wrong moment, the shot will go wild.

Many believers make the same mistake when facing financial problems. Their fear drives them to expect negative experiences. They apply for loans anticipating rejection. They live on the edge of angst, waiting for the next catastrophe to occur. This is the believer's version of "The Flinch," causing one to lose faith-focus when they need to stay on target.

The rifleman overcomes "The Flinch" by keeping his eyes open—by forcing his eyes to remain on his intended target. The Christian keeps himself in faith by focusing on the positive promises of God's Word.

Expecting the worst won't help you receive the

best. Use your force of will to train yourself to expect blessings instead of problems. *"For God is not a man that He should lie, neither is He a son of man that he should change His mind. Has he spoken, and will He not do it, or has He promised and will He not make it good?"*

When faced with financial challenges, don't flinch. Expect the best and God's promise to meet your needs.

PRAYER
Lord, help me to look to you for my daily provision, nightly peace and lasting purpose.

BUILDING BLOCKS OF FAITH
Expect blessings, not problems and your days will be better, not bitter.

Journal

Chapter Eleven

When he looked up he saw the soccer ball skipping across the sand, bouncing off white foam and over the waves. The breeze pushed it beyond the reach of the boy wading toward it. Like a small head floating on the water, the ball turned slowly, the seams turning upwards as if smiling… mocking him.

Rich grabbed the journal and bolted down the steps. The promises of God's provision were a lie, the stories exaggerations written by deranged believers who wouldn't know real financial security if they inherited it. For a few hours he'd believed God cared, led and loved, but no more. He was done with the silly superstitions of simple-minded Christians.

He paused at the water's edge, clutching the journal in his hand. He'd been right all along. There was no God. At least, not a God who mattered. Jesus was just an imaginary friend for those too weak to face the future alone. Gripping the journal by the spine he reached back and sent it flying toward the breakers, pages fluttering like a wounded gull flapping its wings. It hit and sank beneath white foam and the swirl of sand.

For a moment he felt sick to his stomach, the way he had when, as a boy, he'd mowed over his neighbor's flower garden. That had been done in anger, too. And disappointment. He told himself getting rid of the journal was the right thing, that faith in God was a farce. The only thing that really mattered was what could be earned, kept and saved for the future. That was his god and it had never let him down.

He was about to start back to the café when he noticed a slip of stationery lying on the sand near the edge of the tide line. He walked over, picked it up and was about to chunk it into the water when he saw the familiar handwriting. It was the same personalized stationery he'd given Peg for Christmas. Her last one.

He stumbled back and collapsed hard onto the sand, carefully unfolding the letter. Apparently the note had been wedged inside of the journal. How had he missed it? He wondered now if there were other letters in the book, more of Peg's thoughts buried beneath sand and surf.

He began to read.

Dear Rich, if you are reading this then you have the journal. I hope you found it as inspiring as I did. Or maybe you skipped the stories and went straight to the end of the book. I know how you like to be in control, to know how everything will turn out in advance. I suppose that's why you always skip to the last page of a novel to see how it ends. I wish I could tell you how this will end for me but I don't know. The doctors aren't telling me much. I suspect they told you, though. I see the sadness in your eyes even when you laugh.

Please, don't be sad, Rich. No matter what happens, I'll be fine. If I live, I'll live for Christ and if I die I gain eternity with Him. It's a win-win situation and I know how you like those sorts of business deals.

I wish I could give you my faith. I wish you could know the peace I have. I know God is in control. He's led me to this place. And if you let Him, He'll lead you, too. That's the benefit of living by faith, Rich. We get to hear

His voice, feel His hand on our shoulder. We only need to obey when he tells us to go. If you have the journal, then you obeyed. You went. You trusted. I can only hope that means you found Him.

Faith is a gift and it increases the more we trust Him. But first we must take it out and use it. Maybe God's given your small faith a good workout. I hope so. In doing that, He's brought you and me closer. But I do know this. His eyes range throughout the earth to strengthen those whose hearts are faithfully committed to Him, and where He guides, He provides. Whatever you need, Rich, He's already rushing to give you. You only need to ask.

Has He placed you in an impossible situation? Then He is close. He helps when there is no other resource but Him. Great miracles always require acts of submission and total commitment. Faith is believing something will happen before it happens. So let me ask you, Rich. What did you expect to happen? To us? To me? And what do you expect to happen, now?

Sorry, dear, but the nurse just arrived and she's ready to prep me for surgery. But before they begin their work, I have a small request. So small that anyone can do it and yet it will require all your strength.

I want you to give away everything you own. Your business. Your savings. Everything that you depend upon. Just give it away. Do this for me, for us. Then you'll see that He is real. That our faith is real. And that He really cares for us.

If you look up and look around you will

See someone in need, someone who could use the money you have. Give it to them. Give them ALL the money in your wallet. When you do, you'll have what I have. This peace that passes understanding. You'll know then that all things really do work for the good of those that love God, obey His voice, and follow His leading.

Let go of the wealth that is pulling you down. Do it before you drown under its weight. Do this and I'm yours for eternity.

I love you, dear. I hope to see you soon. I mean this afternoon, of course, when you stop by. But later, too, when we stand together on the steps of His Kingdom. I'm reaching my hand out to you. So is God. Let go and take hold. ☺

She signed it "Peg," adding a smiley face the way she had when she signed his birthday, anniversary and Valentine cards.

He hadn't realized he'd been crying until he saw the divots on the sand in the space between his knees. There was no way to get the journal back, of course. But he could honor Peg's wishes.

Carefully folding the letter he stood and stuck it in his pocket. He went striding up the beach toward the boys who'd remained at the water's edge, watching as the wind and tide carried their soccer ball to sea. While he walked, he removed the bills one-by-one.

"In God we trust," Rich said, pointing to the text above the large ONE on the bill. He gave the boys the money and motioned with his foot how they were to spend it. Peg had been right. There was freedom in complete dependence on God. A sense of peace and joy.

Chapter Twelve

Rich lay on a grass pallet in a cabana near the beach. The rustle of palm trees above the bamboo hut fused with the sound of surf. With his eyes still silted over with sleep, he looked past the fluttering flap of the dried goat skin. In the post-dawn glow the green hills of San Juan Del Sur tipped pink, the black slice of Pacific Ocean turned deep blue. The day's first light revealed the compactness of his small home and his meager surroundings. A grass mat, dirt floor and wooden table with a porcelain bowl for washing. Next to the table was the wicker chair he used for reading. His prayer journal lay in the seat atop his Bible. Rolling off his pallet he stood, sliding into a pair of swim trunks.

Outside the cabana he looked toward the rocky path that led toward the beach. Down the hill and past banana trees he saw a larger clearing. A small brown woman carefully stoked a fire beneath a barrel. Nearby clothes dried on a line. Far away a rooster crowed. He gathered his laundry (three tee-shirts, a pair of khakis and two pairs of shorts) and placed it outside his hut.

Once had he offered to wash his own, but only once.

"I can wash, yes? But can I enter Banco del Sur and meet with el jefe over important business matters? No, I cannot. I am only a poor woman who cannot read, but you, Señor Ricardo, understand such things. I will wash. You help our boy to read, no?"

Bending down he hooked the flap over the nail in case it rained. As he did he marveled at the tough brown texture of his bare feet. In the months since he'd walked up the beach and given the young boys money for a new soccer ball, Rich had changed. Both in appearance and attitude.

Gone was the pallid softness and rolls of fat around his waist. He'd always taken a tan easily. Now, with his hair cropped short and bleached white by the sun, his dusty blue eyes were even more intense than before. He did not look like the others, could not match their stamina in the water. But among the others who surfed the waves in front of his cabana, he was the "grande de padre"–Big Papa. It was a term of endearment he treasured.

Tucking the surfboard under his arm he started down the path.

While he walked he thought of that day on the beach. After giving the boys his money he'd walked to the public park in front of the church, unsure of what to do next. Broke and alone, he had expected to feel fear, but instead he'd felt liberated. He sat on a bench and listened to the echo of hoofs striking the cobble-stone streets. The bells of the church chimed. Somewhere nearby, a loud radio played Salsa music.

Peg had been right. Giving away the money had released a weight of worry he hadn't known he'd been carrying. Now he was totally dependent on others. Perhaps this was what the Pastor had meant when he'd said, "Whatever big projects God has planned for you, He will not allow them to move forward until you pass the test in the day of small things." He recalled the nudging he'd felt when he was younger, the promptings to give, and how he'd discounted them. Now he realized that his disobedience had been linked to unbelief.

No more. Now he would act when the small voice spoke.

After praying in the shadow of the church that day, he'd wandered through the village until he passed a surf shop that smelled of resin and fiberglass. He'd stopped to admire the surfboards in the window. In a few minutes one of the young boys from the beach ran up to him bouncing a new soccer ball on his foot. Rich smiled. The boy pointed up the road to an open bed truck crowded with men. The driver waved Rich over and, in very good English, asked if he needed a lift. He needed everything. Food, shelter, a purpose. Climbing up on the running board, he'd clung to the passenger's mirror as they bucked along the rough roads of San Juan Del Sur.

When they'd reached the outskirts of the village a few of the men hopped off the truck. Rich moved to the bed of the truck, sitting on a tire well. He listened to their staccato speech, trying to pick out words he'd heard on the bus, terms he could comprehend. He understood nothing. Soon the driver had to navigate a narrow road that stretched up the mountain. Rich felt the air cool. Howler monkeys hooted from tree tops. More men hopped off until at last, only Rich remained in the back of the truck. When they reached the top of the hill, the driver turned onto a rutted path. Branches slapped the sides of the truck.

They came to the clearing where he stood now. He'd never seen anything so beautiful. The ocean had been cobalt blue that day. Long lines wrapped around a point, bending to form perfect waves that spilled into a small bay. In the distance he'd seen the mountains of Costa Rica. Beyond that, the edge of the world.

Now the ocean was dark, the morning air cool as the breeze blew over the mountain. Wisps of sea spray feathered back as the wind rushed up the face of the waves, breaking over the sand bar. He nodded to the old woman scrubbing a man's blue work shirt. The path curved toward the rocks and with feet bare and toughened by the repetition of these daily walks, he climbed down the sharp ledge, jumping onto the soft sand.

Rich had stayed with the truck driver and his son that evening. The old woman had fed him rice and beans and a large slab of boiled fish. The next morning he'd ridden back down the mountain with the father and son. He'd remained in the village while the other men worked. When the bank opened he'd asked to see the manager.

When the branch manager of Banco del Sur understood the nature of Rich's request, he'd offered Rich the use of a vacant desk and computer terminal. The layout of the keyboard was confusing, but by mid-afternoon he'd transferred all the money in his savings and checking accounts into a new account. The bank official had supervised the transaction. It had taken another week to get the necessary paperwork approved but at last, the San Juan Del Sur Education Endowment had been approved. On the day the trustee of the endowment signed the papers, Rich lost all control to his money. In less than a half hour he'd given away almost a quarter of a million dollars.

The sale of his business had taken longer but at last, that was finished, too. Everything he owned was in the bundle of dirty laundry outside his hut.

The shock of the water stunned him. He still had not grown accustomed to the coolness of water so early in the morning. Or the power of the waves. But the soreness he'd felt the first few days was gone. Now, he, the board and the ocean were one.

He powered through the breakers crashing on the beach and then settled into a steady rhythm as he paddled toward the swells marching toward him. He had learned from the others how to judge the sets and to take advantage of the out-flowing rips that sped him toward the sand bar. Today he would surf alone. The others, the young men and women who waited outside the surf shops for the bus, would be along later. Then the bay would become crowded with surfers. The solitary worship of sitting alone among the beauty of God's creation would be gone. He did not begrudge the younger surfers, though. He was the visitor, the "gringo" who refused to go home. He felt blessed to be called their friend.

He cleared the final wave of a large set and slid into a sitting position, watching the horizon for the pronounced bumps that would signal the next set.

Looking up the hill he saw the smoke wafting through the trees. The man and his son would be up now, preparing to eat breakfast. Rich would only have a few minutes before the honk of the truck's horn called him to work. Today he would purchase the books. Then, if the supplies arrived, he would supervise the unloading of materials. They were coming to the end of the dry season. Soon the monsoon season would arrive, swelling the creeks and making it difficult to lay the foundation of the school. Even God had deadlines, it seemed.

As he turned to catch the wave, he remembered how close he'd come to missing his opportunity, how angry he'd been that Sunday when he'd sat in the Pastor's office. Had it been chance or providence? Maybe he would never know. The back of the board lifted, he sprang to his feet. Dropping down the wave's face, he thought of the final words in the old journal: "Sometimes you just have to take a leap of faith and build your wings on the way down."

The wave fell over him as if the fist of God were squeezing him tight. The barrel narrowed; time slowed. He felt the pulse of the sea, heard the heartbeat of God thumping as surf exploded around him. For a moment, carried along by the power of the ocean, he thought; *So, this is what Jesus meant when He promised that we could have life to the full.*

The sun broke forth. The wave spit him out. Rich snapped a cutback off the face and then rode the spent wave into the beach. The wave walking would have to wait. He had work to do. Kingdom work.

Contributors

Gene Jennings currently serves as Associate Pastor at True North Church in North Augusta, SC. Gene has traveled as a missionary and speaker all over the world, including Australia, Tanzania, Mexico, Costa Rica, and Guatemala. He is a graduate of the University of South Carolina-Aiken and Southwestern Baptist Theological Seminary. Gene's book, *Laughing with Sarah*, is available in stores now. timelywords.blogspot.com

Jan Loy, a freelance writer and speaker, is actively involved in guiding others to greater personal growth. She's authored numerous life application Bible Study Guides, plus created individualized coaching and mentoring programs.

Cindy Sproles is the founder of Mountain Breeze Ministries. She is a contributing writer to *Common Ground Christian Newspaper, Novel Journey and Novel Reviews.* Cindy speaks frequently for ladies' conferences and special events. www.mountainbreezewriter.blogspot.com.

Yvonne Lehman lives in the Blue Ridge Mountains of western North Carolina. She is an award-winning, bestselling author of 40 novels and founder of the Blue Ridge Mountains Christian Writers Conference. www.yvonnelehman.com.

***

Joanna Shumaker is a writer and freelance photographer. Her works have appeared in Catapult Magazine, and Internet Café Devotions. She has written two Ladies Bible Studies entitled, *Renewing Your Spirit* and *The Strong Woman's Guide to a Meek and Quiet Spirit*. Her heart's desire is to encourage women in their mid-life with help and hope for the future through God's message of hope.
www.renewingyourspirit.wordpress.com.

***

Eddie Jones is a three-time winner of the Delaware Christian Writers Conference and author of two nonfiction books. He has written hundreds of columns and articles that have appeared in over 20 different publications. www.eddiejones.org.

***

Sauni Rinehart is a speaker, vocalist, and writer through Triple-E Ministries www.saunirinehart.com. She is also involved in worship arts and women's ministries at her home church. She and her husband make their home in Eastvale.
www.saunirinehart.blogspot.com.

***

Sandy Bradshaw is a freelance writer and Christian motivational speaker. She lives in Kansas where her husband serves as senior pastor of Haysville Christian Church. They have three adult children and two wonderful grandchildren.

Beverly Varnado is a novelist and screenwriter who writes to give people hope in the redemptive purposes of God. She is a 2009 finalist for the Kairos Prize, an international screenplay competition. She was also a finalist in the Gideon Screenplay competition for 2009 and 2008. Her writing credits include the *Upper Room* and a *Focus on the Family* publication. Beverly makes her home with her family and their menagerie of four cats and three dogs. www.beverlyvarnado.com.

Ann Tatlock is the author of the Christy Award-winning novel *All the Way Home*. She has also won the Midwest Independent Publishers Association "Book of the Year" in fiction for both *All the Way Home* and *I'll Watch the Moon*. Her novel *Things We Once Held Dear* received a starred review from Library Journal, and Publishers Weekly calls her "one of Christian fiction's better wordsmiths, and her lovely prose reminds readers why it is a joy to savor her stories."

Irene Brand began writing inspirational novels in 1984. With forty-five books and over two million copies in print, Irene still holds to her grass roots of faith, family and friends. Irene and her husband live in rural West Virginia. www.irenebrand.com.

Cindy Rooy is a columnist in two Tennessee newspapers and has been published in a devotional book titled *Daily Devotions for Writers*. Her Bible study, *Trusting God Through Trouble and Tears*, is being considered for publication. A wife and mother of three grown children, Cindy enjoys a writing and speaking ministry.

Candy Arrington is a contributing writer for Focus on the Family's Focus on Your Child parenting publications. Candy is co-author of *AFTERSHOCK: Help, Hope, and Healing in the Wake of Suicide* and *How to Have a Life While Caring for Your Aging Parent.* www.CandyArrington.com.

Phyllis Qualls Freeman has over two hundred fifty published devotionals, human interest, and other articles. She is working on her first book. Phyllis loves reaching out to touch those who have long-term, life-altering situations to share God's love. Married to her college sweetheart for fifty years, they have three children and five grandchildren.

Sandra M. Hart enjoys writing historical fiction novels set in the Midwest. "Everyday people," she says, inspire her most. She hopes to have a nonfiction book published about a couple of these ordinary heroes who fill our lives with hope.

Cathy Bryant lives in a small Texas town with one amazing husband, two spoiled cats, and a garden full of flowers, hummingbirds and butterflies. www.wordvessel.blogspot.com.

Leah Mix has been married to her wonderful husband, Gary, for 39 years. A transplant from Upstate New York to Florida, Leah experienced culture shock, but now loves her home and wouldn't want to live anywhere else. She found out that when God plants you, He will make you happy blooming there. Leah is the mother of two and grandmother of five. Writing is a new venture for Leah, but has been a dream for years. She is excited about the future because she has found, God is good - all the time.

Andrea Merrell is a freelance writer and editor with a passion to help others see God's Word as practical and relevant for ordinary, everyday life. She has written material for ladies' groups, marriage retreats, skits, websites, and brochures, and is currently working on three novels and countless devotions. Andrea is a staff writer and copy editor for www.ChristianDevotions. us and www.DevoKids.com, and lives in South Carolina with her husband (and best friend), Charlie. www.andreamerrell.com.

Danny Woodall lives in Port Neches, TX. He and his wife have three children. He has a monthly column in Christian Online Magazine, and has written for *Life Way's Essential Connections* and *Bible Express* magazines. This past year he contributed to *Daily Devotions for Writers*. He and his wife, Arlene, work with the fourth grade Sunday school.

Shelby Rawson is an active leader in her church's Mom's Together program and facilitates Soul Care groups. She's the author of *Daddy Do You Love Me: A Daughter's Journey of Faith and Restoration*, as well as the *Parents of Preschoolers Web Content Manager for Next Generation Institute*.

Loree Lough has authored 68 books, 59 short stories, and more than 2,500 articles. Her works have won dozens of awards. Several of her novellas have appeared in collections that made it onto the Christian Booksellers Association bestseller lists. www.loreelough.com.

Jennifer Landsberger was an Engineering Laboratory Technician (nuclear chemist) in the U.S. Navy. She's a member of the American Christian Fiction Writers. She has completed one book and is working on her second. Jennifer enjoys writing devotionals, articles, and short stories.

David Loy is an aspiring writer, with hopes of impacting and encouraging the lives of those around him. He is married to Stephanie, and lives in Thompsons Station, TN. His parents are skilled and accomplished writers/teachers, and they are his inspiration in terms of writing and in his Faith.

Pat Jeanne Davis is a homemaker and writer living in Philadelphia, Pa. Her essays, stories and articles have appeared in *The Lookout, GRIT Magazine, The Mennonite, Renewed* and *Ready, Guideposts, Chicken Soup for the Soul, Blessings for Mothers, God Answers Prayer, Woman Alive, Woman's Touch*. She has completed an inspirational historical novel.

Kelli Regan passionately shares her message of Christ with others through writing, leading a Bible study, prison ministry and one-on-one encounters. She and her husband reside in Bucks County, PA with their two children where she's a self-employed writer and graphic designer. www.awesomegodordinarygirl.blogspot.com.

Kristi Buttles is a freelance writer and photographer involved in several ministries in her home church. She has written fiction, non-fiction, a Bible study, and a children's book which she also illustrated. She has designed her own line of unique greeting cards that combine her love for words and her passion for photography.

Dr. Christopher Stocklin is the founder of Turning the Tide Financial Ministries established in 2007. Chris and his wife, Carol, travel throughout the country conducting Financial Victory Conferences in churches. The goal of the ministry is introducing a Biblical approach to personal money management in the home. Dr. Stocklin has written *Cash, Credit, and Control* and recently released financial workbook *Turning Your Finances Right-Side Up...After Being Turned Up-Side Down*. www.turningthetideministries.com.

Miralee Ferrell heads the local chapter of American Christian Fiction Writers serving the Portland, Oregon -Vancouver, Washington area. Miralee is a published author in both women's contemporary fiction and historical romance. She's married and has two children, loves to garden, read, ride horses and sail with her husband.

DiAnn Mills has over forty books in print and has sold a million and a half copies. Six of her anthologies have appeared on the CBA Best Seller List. Three of her books have won the distinction of Best Historical of the Year by Heartsong Presents. She was a Christy Awards finalist in 2008. She speaks to various groups and teaches writing workshops around the country. DiAnn is also a mentor for Jerry B. Jenkins Christian Writer's Guild.

Susan Dollyhigh is a freelance writer, columnist and winner of the Women in Faith Shine the Light Contest. She's also a 2009 Blue Ridge Mountains Christian Writers Conference winner.

Virginia Smith writes mystery/suspense novels and in 2008 won the Writer of the Year award at the Mount Hermon Christian Writer's Conference. Her novels include *Bluegrass Peril, A Taste of Murder, Stuck in the Middle, Sister-to-Sister Series,* and *Sincerely, Mayla.* www.VirginiaSmith.org.

Tina Givens has a passion for encouraging people through her writing and singing. In addition to writing devotional pieces, Tina writes articles and advertising copy as marketing manager for NRB Network, a Christian educational and informational television channel seen nationwide on DIRECTV. Tina lives in Jacksonville, Florida, where she sings with the group Deliberate Praise and is a member of First Coast Christian Writers.

***

David Stearman is a novelist, recording artist, and missionary to various European, Asian, and Latin American countries. His stories describe the remote corners of the world and the people who inhabit them as only a physical and cultural eyewitness can. He travels extensively within US borders as well, offering encouragement to the believers in numerous and diverse churches. When home, he and his wife Diane reside in Louisville, KY.

***

Pat Davis is a homemaker and writer living in Philadelphia, Pa. Her essays, stories and articles have appeared in The *Lookout, GRIT Magazine, The Mennonite, Renewed and Ready, Guideposts, Chicken Soup for the Soul, Blessings for Mothers, God Answers Prayer, Woman Alive,* and *Woman's Touch.* She has completed an inspirational historical novel.

You Can Help

Create a personalized version of
Faith and FINANCES: In God We Trust
for your church. Here's how.

Church Outreach Ministries

By working with the church staff and its outreach committees, we will mix testimonies from congregational members alongside devotions from best-selling Christian authors, thus creating a "one off" book that's unique to that church. When completed, this personalized version of *Faith* **and FINANCES: In God We Trust** can be used as an outreach tool, small group study, Sunday school curriculum or fund-raising gift. Churches will find this book to be a great way to launch a building campaign, reduce debt, and teach stewardship. Congregational members can purchase copies at a discounted price and distribute them to nursing homes, hospitals, shut-ins, and new members, extending the message of God's care and concern of our finances beyond the walls of the building.

Missions Fund Raising

Faith **and FINANCES: In God We Trust** is also a great way to help youth groups earn funds for ongoing missions trips or projects within their church. *Faith* **and FINANCES: In God We Trust** can be personalized with devotions from teens and young adults, giving youth an opportunity to, not only be published, but raise funds for travel expenses.

Small Group Study

Finally, ***Faith* and FINANCES: In God We Trust** can be used as a small group study. Ministers will find the book useful in counseling couples, families and anyone struggling to cast off the golden handcuffs and live the abundant life Jesus promised. On our web site you will find our ***Faith* and FINANCES: Field Manual.** www.FaithandFinances.us

How can you help?

1. Introduce ***Faith* and FINANCES: In God We Trust** to your congregation and mission committees. Encourage your church family to consider using ***Faith* and FINANCES: In God We Trust** as a mission tool or fund raising item. (We offer deep discounts to churches that purchase in bulk.)

2. Tell at least three people about ***Faith* and FINANCES: In God We Trust**. Encourage them to purchase a copy online at: www.faithandfinances.us or the ministry: books@christiandevotions.us.

3. Tell your friends to visit, www.faithandfinances.us, and take the ***Faith* & FINANCES** challenge. Each week we update the site with testimonials of how God has provided for and prodded the hearts, wallets and purses of readers.

4. Write a book review for your local paper, blog, church web site, personal web site or online at Amazon.com. Search for the title of the book, then scroll down and click to add your review. Potential readers do read Amazon reviews, so this is a great way to help.

5. Do you know someone who hosts an online radio show, or works in traditional media? Ask them to invite us to be on their show. We can be reached at: cindy@christiandevotions.us.

6. If you own a retail business, consider putting a display of these books on your counter to resell to customers. If you work with a ministry or church, ask them to purchase several copies to be used as gifts, recruitment tools, or study guides. In the past, we've had companies purchase large quantities of our books to give to their new employees. This is a great way to spread the seeds of faith.

7. Invite us to speak to your church, group or community. In early 2010 we'll begin booking venues for our nationwide book tour. We'd love to visit your city. Contact Cindy to get us on your calendar; cindy@ christiandevotions.us.

Finally, pray for the success of this book and that God will use it to its full potential. The success of **Faith and FINANCES: In God We Trust** depends on your belief in this ministry and your personal dedication and prayers. We believe that God has inspired our writers and our ministry to bring this book into fruition. We pray for your support as well.

At a time when our nation is suffering financially, families need to practice the motto of our currency and, Trust In God. We hope this book will begin to turn the hearts of a nation back toward God one paycheck at a time.

Would you like to be a host "home" for our progressive "dinner" book tour?

As part of the book launch, we're inviting our blogging friends to participate in our virtual book tour. We will provide the meal: an excerpt from the book, an article specific to YOUR site, a short interview from one of the authors in the book, video clip, guest contest giveaway, sample questions from the study guide, and more.

As host, you will receive a free copy of: *Faith* **and FINANCES: In God We Trust**, *A Journey to Financial Dependence*. Won't you help turn the hearts of a nation back toward God?

Contact us at books@christiandevotions.us.

CPSIA information can be obtained at www.ICGtesting.com
Printed in the USA
LVOW062333140413

329042LV00001B/21/P